THE CHOICE IS YOURS

...OR IS IT?

A Deeper Look at the Sovereignty of God and the Free Will of Man

JOHN MARINELLI

TABLE OF CONTENTS

PREFACE

I authored this book because many of my friends believed that what happened to them resulted from God's sovereign will and not their personal choices. I realized God was being blamed for many things he did not do. I intend to disprove that premise and unveil the truth of God's word.

I investigated God's sovereignty and man's free will. Does man have the freedom to make choices or is he just acting out the sovereign will of his creator? We will examine both sides of this proverbial coin in the coming chapters.

I will use the KJV of the Bible and some good old basic logic in my quest to discover the truth. I will also call attention to heretical teachings and false doctrines that are currently attacking the church today.

The question set before us is, "Is It My Choice or Not?

INTRODUCTION

Why did God create man? Was it because he wanted a robotic vessel that he could program to do his bidding? Are some folks programmed to be bad and others good? If that is so, is God's character both good and evil?

Am I in control of my destiny or is my destiny controlled by me? Is it all planned out already and I am just a pawn in a much larger scheme? Sometimes I feel like I have no control over my life. Do you feel that way?

This book takes a deeper look at "Free Will" and the "Sovereignty of God." These two doctrines have been a source of controversy in the church for centuries. Is God in control, or am I? Can we both be in control at the same time?

Let us look at the sovereignty of God through the teachings of John Calvan, a 6th-century French Reform theologian first and then at man's free will. These two doctrinal teachings have split denominations, destroyed fellowships and even today cause new believers to stumble in their Christian walk.

It is time to set the record straight, tell the truth, and expose centuries of errors. I realize I am presenting my understanding of the subject. However, this is over 60 years of study, Bible research, and prayer. It ought to be worth the reading.

CHAPTER ONE:
THE SOVEREIGNTY
OF GOD AND TOTAL
DEPRAVITY

The **Sovereignty of God** is the theological assumption. It says that all things are under God's rule and control and that nothing happens without his direction. God works, not just some things, but all things, according to the counsel of his own will (see Eph. 1:11). His purposes are all-inclusive and never thwarted (see Isa. 46:11); nothing takes him by surprise. The sovereignty of God is not merely that God has the power to govern all things, but that he does so, always and without exception. God is not merely sovereign in principle, but also sovereign in practice.

"Although the sovereignty of God is universal and absolute, it is not the sovereignty of blind power. Coupled with infinite wisdom, holiness, and love, sovereignty embodies a universal and absolute power. And this doctrine, when properly understood, is most comforting. Who would not prefer his or her affairs to be in the hands of a God of infinite power, wisdom, holiness, and love? The alternative is to have them left to fate, chance, or irrevocable natural law, or to shortsighted and perverted self. Those who reject God's sovereignty should consider what alternatives they have left." Loraine Boettner, author of Reformed Doctrine of Predestination.

God created all beings, including the angels, but some have fallen. Let us be sure that this does not make God the author of sin, for, as man, they fell from their created state. This includes all false gods. But God is over them, whether they be angels, demons, or the god of this world, the devil.

A man may fight against God, but he cannot win. God often uses evil men to accomplish his will in battle. Jesus is said to have been slain from the foundation of the world, and the cross is one of the most credible pieces of evidence of God's sovereignty.

"Crucify him," "Crucify him", was their cry, but when they nailed him to the cross, they did not realize they were fulfilling God's will for his Son. Peter said, "him (Christ), being delivered by the determinate counsel and foreknowledge of God, ye have taken and by wicked hands have crucified and slain." Acts 2:23. But this God of all power was not defeated in this evil act, for the Lord Jesus was raised from the dead. By it, the devil was defeated and all his ministers of (self) righteousness. This is a great example of God's sovereignty in action.

The Psalmist said, "*Thou are exalted far above all gods,*" Psalm 97:9, And again, "*Our Lord is above all gods,*" Psalm 135.5, "*O give thanks unto the God of gods.*" Psalm 136.2.

Our God cannot fail, lie, or sin. Neither is he frustrated at man's failure. God is the author of his sovereign grace and mercy.

"For he saith to Moses, I will have mercy on whom I will have mercy, and I will have compassion on whom I will have compassion. So, it is not of him that wills, nor of him that runs, but of God that shows mercy... And whom he will, he hardens." (Rom. 9:15-16, 18.)

Judas, who betrayed Jesus, had betrayed himself and met his just due. John wrote, "Jesus knew from the beginning who should betray him. And he said,

"No man can come unto me, except it were given unto him of my Father ... Have not I chosen you twelve, and one of you is a devil (i.e., slanderer) ... He spoke of Judas ... for he it was that should betray him, being one of the twelve." (John 6:64-71.)

Many Christians have doubts about God's sovereignty. Yet there is one aspect of the Christian life where they profess, maybe unknowingly, that God is sovereign. They said as many do, "God has done all he can do. Now the rest is up to you."

How contradictory! They may stand on their feet and deny this blessed, comforting, enabling doctrine, but when they bend their knees in prayer, asking God to save them, do they not realize they are calling on a sovereign God, whom only he has the right and the ability to save?

The question is, If God has done all that he can do, why pray to him? But we pray knowing he is the only one who can do what man cannot otherwise do. This power belongs to God, and not man. (Excerpts from Sovereign Grace Baptist Proclaimer)

The current doctrine of sovereignty emerged over five centuries ago. It is the Protestant theological system that fosters predestination. Calvinism, as the doctrine is called, was the theology of John Calvin, a French theologian and Protestant reformer in the 16th century.

Those who follow this "Predestination" theology believe that God, in his sovereign rule, saved some of humanity and damn the rest. They are commonly known as "Hyper-Calvinists." Their viewpoint includes justification by faith alone, with emphasis on the grace of God. The doctrine of predestination, which holds that God has already determined who will be saved and who will be damned, is a key tenet of John Calvin's teachings.

Calvinism has had a significant impact on the development of Western culture and has influenced many aspects of modern society.

This acrostic will help us remember the Calvinistic doctrine, TULIP.

T- Total depravity

U- Unconditional Election

L- Limited Atonement

Irresistible Grace

P- Perseverance of the saints

It is important to know this stuff. Most of the Protestant movement is based upon it. Most folks cannot quote the TULIP acrostic, but they believe and practice it just the same. Here is a description of the acrostic letters:

Total Depravity…means complete, not partial. It is total. When someone is depraved, they live in a quality or state that is corrupt or perverted. Here are some synonyms of depravity: abjection, corruption, corruptness, debasement, debauchery, decadence, decadency, degeneracy, degenerateness, degeneration, degradation, demoralization, dissipatedness, dissipation, dissoluteness, libertinage, libertinism, perversion, perverseness, rakishness, and turpitude.

From the Christian perspective, depravity means sin, sinfulness, unrighteous, ungodly, and evil.

Note: The teaching says there is no escape from this state of being. It is total and complete in every form. We cannot just do or get better on our own. The condition is permanent and final. It came to us through Adam and his fall from grace. (See Romans 5:12)

The implications of such a condition are:

- We can do good works, but they will not change the underlying condition of depravity. "As it is written: "There is none righteous, no, not one; There is none who understands; There is none who seeks after God. They have all turned aside; They have all together become unprofitable; There is none who does good, no, not one." Romans 3:10.

- We can try to be good and even claim to be righteous, but that will not make us better. "The heart *is* deceitful above all things and desperately wicked: who can know it?" Jeremiah 17:9.

- Man's righteousness misses the mark. **Isaiah 64:6** said, "all our righteousness is like filthy rags." The Pharisees had righteousness, but Jesus asserts that our righteousness must exceed theirs (Matthew 5:20), meaning that we need to have his righteousness imputed to us, which becomes our new covering, our new garment.

- We were born dead, dead to God, and lost. "And you *hath he quickened,* who were dead in trespasses and sins; Wherein in time past ye walked according to the course of this world, according to the prince of the power of the air, the spirit that now works in the children of disobedience: Among whom also we all had our conversation in times past in the lusts of our flesh, fulfilling the desires of the flesh and the mind; and were by nature the children of wrath, even as others. But God, who is rich in mercy, for his great love wherewith he loved us, even when we were dead in sins, hath quickened us together with Christ, (by grace ye are saved;) And hath raised us up together, and made us sit together in heaven-ly places in Christ Jesus." Ephesians 2:1-7.

The next letter in our acrostic is "U" which continues the teaching. By the time we get through the TULIP acrostic, you will clearly understand the John Calvin teachings.

Note: I want to go on record as being opposed to most of what is presented and consider much of it as heresy. This book is all about what makes John Calvin's message false and destructive to the Christian experience. As we go beyond Calvinism into Arminian theology, we will also encounter heresy that distorts the simplicity of the gospel message. I will offer my rebuttal as we discuss each subject.

CHAPTER TWO:
THE SOVEREIGNTY OF GOD AND UNCONDITIONAL ELECTION

We cannot ignore the concept of "Election" when discussing the sovereignty of God. They go together like bread and butter.

The act of God referred to as "election" in the Bible is when he chose those who will be saved. The Bible repeatedly teaches this doctrine. According to the scriptures, before salvation, all individuals are spiritually dead in sin (Ephesians 2:1-3). In this state of death, the sinner is utterly unable to respond to any spiritual stimulus and therefore unable to love God, obey him, or please him. The scripture said the mind of every unbeliever "is hostile toward God; for it does not subject itself to the law of God, for it cannot do so; and those who are in the flesh cannot please God" (Romans 8:7-8).

That describes a state of total hopelessness: spiritual death. The effect of all this is that no sinner can ever make the first move in the salvation process. This is what Jesus meant in John 6:44, when he said, "No one can come to me unless the Father who sent me draws him." This is also why the Bible repeatedly stresses that salvation is wholly God's work.

Note: *(I believe God can speak to the dead and they will hear and respond accordingly.) I see this in Ezekiel, chapter 37. Take a read:*

THE VALLEY OF DRY BONES …EZEKIEL 37

"The hand of the Lord was on me, and he brought me out by his Spirit and set me down in the middle of the valley; it was full of bones. He led me all around them. There were a great many of them on the surface of the valley, and they were very dry. Then he said to me, "Son of man, can these bones live? "

I replied, "Lord God, only you know."

He said to me, "Prophesy concerning these bones and say to them: Dry bones, hear the word of the Lord! This is what the Lord God says to these bones: I will cause breath to enter you, and you will live. I will put tendons on you, make flesh grow on you, and cover you with skin. I will put breath in you so that you come to life. Then you will know that I am the Lord."

So I prophesied as I had been commanded. While I was prophesying, there was a noise, a rattling sound, and the bones came together, bone to bone. As I looked, tendons appeared on them, flesh grew, and skin covered them, but there was no breath in them. He said to me, "Prophesy to the breath, prophesy, son of man. Say to it: This is what the Lord God says: Breath, come from the four winds and breathe into these slain so that they may live!" So I prophesied as he commanded me; the breath entered them, and they came to life and stood on their feet, a vast army."

I realize this text focuses on the restoration of Israel. However, the fact that God can use man to speak to dry bones (The dead) whether physical or spiritual is event. He is referring to spiritually dead folks that are that came alive. Isn't that what God does to the "Totally Depraved" soul? He is not only able, but does call them back to life.

Steve Lawson of ligonier.org says this in his recent article on election. (I present this article so you can see how the Calvinists think. *(My comments are in the paragraph above.)*

The idea that God does what he wants, and that what he does is true and right because he does it, is foundational to our understanding of everything in scripture, including the doctrine of election.

In the broad sense, election refers to the fact that God chooses (or elects) to do everything that he does in whatever way he sees fit. When he acts, he does so only because he willfully and independently chooses to act. According to his own nature, predetermined plan, and good pleasure, he does whatever he desires, without pressure or constraint from any outside influence.

The Bible makes this point repeatedly. In the act of Creation, God made precisely what he wanted to create in the way he wanted to create it (cf. Gen. 1:31). And ever since Creation, he has sovereignly prescribed or permitted everything in human history, so that he might accomplish the redemptive plan that he previously had designed (cf. Isa. 25:1; 46:10; 55:11; Rom. 9:17; Eph. 3:8–11).

In the Old Testament, he chose a nation for himself. Out of all the nations in the world, he selected Israel (Deut. 7:6; 14:2; Psalms. 105:43; 135:4). He chose the Israelites, not because they were better or more desirable than any other people, but simply because he decided to choose them. In the words of Richard Wolf, "How odd of God to choose the Jews." It might not have rhymed as well, but the same would have been true of any other people God might have selected. God chooses whomever he chooses for reasons that are wholly his.

The nation of Israel was not the only recipient in the scripture of God's electing choice. In the New Testament, Jesus Christ is called 'My Chosen One" (Luke 9:35). The holy angels also are referred to as "elect angels" (1 Tim. 5:21). And New Testament believers are called "God's chosen ones" (Col. 3:12; cf. 1 Cor. 1:27; 2 Thess. 2:13; 2 Tim. 2:10; Titus 1:1; 1 Peter 1:1; 2:9; 5:13; Rev. 17:14), meaning that the church is a community of those who were chosen, or "elect" (Eph. 1:4).

When Jesus tells his disciples, 'You did not choose me, but I chose you" (John 15:16), He was underscoring this truth. And the New Testament reiterates it in passage after passage. Acts 13:48b describes salvation in these words: "As many as were appointed to eternal life believed." Ephesians 1:4–6 notes that God "chose us in [Christ] before the foundation of the world, that we should be holy and blameless before him. In love he predestined us for adoption through Jesus Christ, according to the purpose of his will, to the praise of his glorious grace, with which he has blessed us in the Beloved."

In his letters to the Thessalonians, Paul reminded his readers that he knew God's choice of them (1 Thess. 1:4) and that he was thankful for them "because God chose you as the first fruits to be saved" (2 Thess. 2:13). The Word of God is clear: believers are those whom God chose for salvation from before the beginning.

The foreknowledge to which Peter refers (1 Peter 1:2) should not be confused with simple foresight. Some teach this view, contending that God, in eternity past, looked down the halls of history to see who would respond to his call and then elected the redeemed on the basis of their response.

(God has no halls of history. He is everywhere at every time and because of that, he can know in advance the decisions of man. Foreknowledge is foreknowledge. It's all about knowing in advance. It is not rocket science.)

Such an explanation makes God's decision subject to man's decision and gives man a level of sovereignty that belongs only to God. It makes God the One who is passively chosen rather than One who actively chooses. And it misunderstands the way in which Peter uses the term foreknowledge. In 1 Peter 1:20, the apostle uses the verb form of that word, prognosis in the Greek, to refer to Christ. In that case, the concept of "foreknowledge" certainly includes the idea of a deliberate choice. It is reasonable, then, to conclude that the same is true when Peter applies prognosis to believers in other places (cf. 1 Peter 1:2).

(Free Will does not negate sovereignty. It only says that God wanted beings

that would be on his level…in his image and likeness. Thus, man was given the power of choice by God, even if those choices would fight against his sovereignty. That's why Jesus said the road to salvation would be narrow and few would find it…because many rebelled against God's sovereignty to go their own way.)

The ninth chapter of Romans also reiterates the elective purposes of God. There, God's electing prerogative is clearly displayed in reference to his saving love for Jacob (and Jacob's descendants) as opposed to Esau (and Esau's lineage). God chose Jacob over Esau, not on the basis of anything Jacob or Esau had done, but according to his own free and uninfluenced sovereign purpose. To those who might protest, "That is unfair!" Paul simply asked, "Who are you, O man, to answer back to God?" (v. 20).

Many more scripture passages could be added to this survey. Yet, as straightforward as the Word of God is, people continually have difficulty accepting the doctrine of election. The reason, again, is that they allow their preconceived notions of how God should act (based on a human definition of fairness) to override the truth of his sovereignty as laid out in the scriptures.

Frankly, the only reason to believe in election is because it is found explicitly in God's Word. No man and no committee of men originated this doctrine. It is like the doctrine of eternal punishment, in that it conflicts with the dictates of the carnal mind. It is repugnant to the sentiments of the unregenerate heart. Like the doctrine of the Holy Trinity and the miraculous birth of our Savior, the truth of election, because it has been revealed by God, must be embraced with simple and unquestioning faith. If you have a Bible and you believe it, you have no option but to accept what it teaches.

The Word of God presents God as the controller and disposer of all creatures (Dan. 4:35; Isa. 45:7; Lam. 3:38), the Most High (Psalms. 47:2; 83:18), the ruler of heaven and earth (Gen. 14:19; Isa. 37:16), and the One against whom none can stand (2 Chron. 20:6; Job 41:10; Isa. 43:13). He is the Almighty who works all things after the counsel of his will (Eph.

1:11; cf. Isa. 14:27; Rev. 19:6) and the heavenly Potter who shapes men according to His own good pleasure (Rom. 9:18–22). In short, He is the decider and determiner of every man's destiny, and the controller of every detail in each individual's life (Prov. 16:9; 19:21; 21:1; cf. Ex. 3:21–22; 14:8; Ezra 1:1; Dan. 1:9; James 4:15)—which is really just another way of saying, "He is God."

Understand that electron is an obvious example of God's sovereignty. However, there are other views on the subject which we will also discuss. I can sum up all of what I have presented so far in this statement...God's choice to redeem humanity has no limitations. You cannot add, "Subject to," anything for it to work. This viewpoint eliminates free will choices and places salvation solely at the desecration of God in accordance with his own will.

(If you eliminate free will, you also eliminate image and likeness from the creation of man. He was created that way and that must include free will as well as sovereignty. I see nothing wrong with man being able to do as he pleases, just like God does. That is being sovereign...to rule over his own life. Adam chose that path in life and rebelled, but God knew it from the beginning. It was an act of free will based upon his own personal sovereignty.)

People refer to those who are chosen as the 'elect' because that word signifies "determining beforehand," "ordaining," and "deciding ahead of time." In simpler terms, it means that even before this world came into existence, God had already determined who would receive salvation.

FIVE SIGNS THAT YOU ARE ONE OF GOD'S ELECT

(Taken from Scripture Savvy Commentary)

How do you know you are among the "Elect or Chosen" of God?" While the concept of predestination can be difficult to grasp, the Bible gives us some indications of how we can know if we are among the elect. Here are some signs that may indicate that you are one of God's chosen:

1. Spiritual Fruit

A fundamental sign of being one among the elect is the manifestation of spiritual fruit in your life. The book of Galatians (5:22-23) explicitly mentions these fruits, which comprise love, joy, peace, patience, kindness, goodness, faithfulness, gentleness, and self-control.

Should you observe these qualities flourishing in your life, it may be an outward expression that God's Spirit is operating within you.

2. Perseverance

Perseverance is another hallmark of being one of the elect. Salvaged individuals will continue to hold on to their faith and perform good deeds until their earthly lives end. To be sure, it does not mean that they will never encounter struggles or transgressions, but rather that they will ultimately endure and persist in their faith.

3. Repentance

Repentance likewise stands as a sign of the work of God's grace in our lives. The presence of divine grace within us will convict our souls of our sins, enabling us to repent and turn away from them.

As a result, we will have an unrelenting desire to lead a life that brings honor and glory to God, reflecting his attributes.

4. Love for God and his Word

Those who are among the elect will have a love for God and his Word. They will desire to spend time in prayer and studying the Bible, and they will seek to obey God's commands.

5. Confirmation by the Holy Spirit

Ultimately, the Holy Spirit confirms to us that we are among the elect. According to Romans 8:16, the Spirit testifies with our spirit that we are God's children.

Such a confirmation is not merely a subjective feeling but stems from the

Holy Spirit's workings in our hearts, resulting in deep-seated conviction within us.

Although it is impossible to be fully sure if we are among the elect, we may look for signs of God's grace actively working within us. The presence of spiritual fruit, perseverance, repentance, love for God and his word, and confirmation by the Holy Spirit may be indicative of our status as the chosen ones.

(It is not impossible to know that you are saved, sealed, and being delivered. See Romans 8:15-16 and I John 5:13. They are very clear on this matter.)

Regardless of whether we are among the elect, we can trust in the goodness and sovereignty of God and his plan for our lives.

The Biblical concepts of "chosen" and "elect" are words that are utilized interchangeably by many individuals, although they may hold different connotations at times.

The word "chosen" generally refers to an idea of selection or preference, such as in Deuteronomy 7:6, which explained that God has chosen the Israelites to be his prized possession among all peoples. This reference to being chosen highlights the fact that Israel is set apart for God's purposes.

The term "elect," on the other hand, has a more detailed significance – it represents being predestined for salvation. In Romans 8:33, Paul writes that those whom God has chosen cannot be accused because it is God who justifies. Here, the meaning of "chosen" is more like being elected for salvation.

While the use of the terms "chosen" and "elect" may convey slightly different connotations, the Bible emphasizes our salvation rests on God's unfettered choice rather than on our individual merits or efforts. Whether we use the notion of "chosen" or "elect," the fact remains – our redemption is ultimately an act of God's grace.

In Ephesians 1:4-5, Paul writes that God "chose us in him before the creation of the world to be holy and blameless in his sight. In love, he predestined us for adoption to sonship through Jesus Christ, in accordance with his pleasure and will." In this verse, the words "chosen" and "predestined" are used interchangeably to stress that our salvation is solely based on God's pre-determined choice.

Note: "Unconditional Election", even with its predestination feature, does not foster eternal security. The Calvinists that I know told me they never can be sure they are among the "Elect" because God made his choices before the world was, and maybe he did not include them. They say that they can only persevere and hope. This is what is called an erroneous conclusion.

There are issues with this way of thinking that need to be looked at. They are:

- If man does not possess "Free Will," we can only conclude that God is the one who causes and accomplishes everything that happens. It is part of his sovereignty.

- The source of evil does not come from evil people that choose to do evil but from God, who controls all that happens.

- God is responsible for all the bad that happens in life because he allowed it to take place and does not step in to prevent it.

- If we are to put on the whole armor of God to defend ourselves against evil forces, isn't that setting up a scenario where God is fighting himself. He is responsible for every action because his creation has no "free will" and, therefore, no responsibility.

- If man has no responsibility for his own actions, how can he be judged for what he does wrong?

CHAPTER THREE: THE SOVEREIGNTY OF GOD AND LIMITED ATONEMENT

The Calvinistic view of salvation is; God has limited his atonement to a select few, in particular, those who he chose before the foundation of the world. The rest of humanity remains lost and bound for hell. Billions will live, die, and burn forever. People consider the rationale for such an act to be merciful. (Go figure!) This viewpoint brings up several questions:

- Why does God create to destroy?
- Why subject the "Elect" to the anger of the dammed?
- Why limit salvation to a select few in the 1ˢᵗ place?
- Why deny the masses access to divine grace?

The doctrine of limited atonement is the third of the Five Points of Calvinism and is represented by the letter *L* in the word *TULIP,* the word we use to help us remember the Five Points and their order.

This doctrine has been given other names. It is sometimes spoken of as the doctrine of particular atonement or of particular redemption. For the same reasons, it is sometimes called definite redemption.

It is also, so it seems, the most difficult of the five points to receive and believe as the teaching of the scriptures, though they certainly do teach this doctrine. It is, for this reason, often rejected by those who are Calvinistic in their other teachings, so that there are some who claim to be four-point Calvinists, accepting the other four points and rejecting this one. This, to be sure, is really an impossibility, since all five of these doctrines "hang together" and are impossible to separate from one another. Nevertheless, the fact that some attempt to be four-point Calvinists does show the difficulty of this doctrine.

It is certainly regrettable that this is so, since this doctrine concerns the work of Christ on the cross and the benefits of that work for God's people. What ought to be a source of fellowship and of unity and of mutual faith in the death and redemptive work of Jesus Christ has become instead a matter of division and even strife among those who believe differently. Let it be clear that it is not our intent in treating this doctrine to further that strife or cause division, but to show as clearly as possible the teaching of the scriptures in the hope that this may further unity and fellowship in the truth.

(Many have called "Limited Atonement" heresy because it contradicts the Whosoever" theology of John 3:16)

The doctrine of limited atonement teaches that Christ died only for some persons, a "limited" number of persons. Those who teach this doctrine would agreed that the "limitation" on the atonement is election, in other words, that Christ died only for the elect and that it is only the elect who benefit from Christ's death.

Some clarification is needed here, for most of those who believe in a universal atonement do not believe that everyone benefits from the death of Christ in the sense that everyone is finally saved. They believe that Christ died for every person and that salvation is made available to everyone through the death of Christ, and they are those who believe and benefit fully from Christ's death.

On the other hand, those who believe in limited atonement do not teach that the power and value of Christ's death is in any way limited. The only thing limited is the number of those for whom Christ died, and the limitation is not due to any defect in the work or death of Christ but to God's sovereign decree to save some and not others. For this reason, many who teach and believe in limited atonement prefer to speak of "particular atonement" rather than "limited atonement," since the word *particular* much more accurately describes what they believe, i.e., that Christ died only for particular persons and not for all people. The word *particular* also leaves no doubt about what exactly is limited here. (This explanation is from the Protestant Reformed Church of America)

Note: *The question is...Is salvation limited or universal?* If it is limited to only the Jews, which would be "His people" as the scripture seems to show, why evangelize the entire world? Why did Peter reach out to the gentiles? Why did Jesus tell his followers to go into the entire world and preach the gospel? Wouldn't they be preaching in vain? I guess the real question is, who are "His People" that he came to save from their sins?

Some folks that hold to this doctrine say that if we challenge it, we are fighting against God and the scriptures. However, a closer look is justified to be sure the interpretation is correct. There are too many questions for it to be an accurate interpretation.

I must also consider the "Whosoever" doctrine of salvation as Jesus presented to Nicodemus in John 3:16. Whosoever refers to whomever, meaning, anyone, that believes, not just a select few or group. There is also God's word to Abraham in genesis that spoke of making him the father of many nations, not just one.

Here is one last example that contradicts limited atonement. It comes straight from the Bible. "For God did not send his Son into the world to condemn the world, but to save the world through him." **1 Timothy 1:15.** The world is more than just a small group of folks in the middle east. It includes every creature, as Jesus said in the great commission. (Matthew 28)

CHAPTER FOUR: THE SOVEREIGNTY OF GOD AND IRRESISTIBLE GRACE

(An Article From Truth Magazine Makes It All Clear)

It is true that certain physical blessings of the grace of God are given to the believer and unbeliever alike. Jesus said, "For he makes the sun to rise on the evil and on the good, and sends rain on the just and the unjust." (Matt. 5:45) Paul explained in I Tim. 4: 10 that God "is the Savior of all men," i.e., God sustains all life upon this earth through the bestowal of certain physical blessings (e.g., sunshine, rain, air, etc.). No one denies this.

Notice, however, what Paul next said, "For therefore we both labor and suffer reproach, because we trust in the living God, who is the Savior of all men, specially of those who believe. " Paul, in the last clause of v. 10, is speaking of the spiritual blessings of God which contributed to the eternal salvation of man. This grace is given to believers. (All men, including believers, kills limited atonement.)

Calvinism denies that any "special grace is shown to believers as opposed to unbelievers. The doctrine of "irresistible grace" is a branch off the vine of "predestination." God's grace to salvation, according to Calvinism, is given only to the elect-whether the elect desire it or not. The Presbyterian Confession of Faith states: "This effectual call is of God's free and special grace alone, not from anything at all foreseen in man, who is altogether passive therein, until, being quickened and renewed by the Holy Spirit, he is thereby enabled to answer this call, and to embrace the grace offered and conveyed in it."

This doctrine, as you can see, provides for a direct and mysterious indwelling of the Spirit. This doctrine, together with its foundation doctrine (predestination), teaches that an "elected" person is saved at the very beginning in the mind of God, and he is saved "in fact" when God arbitrarily sends his Spirit into the heart of that individual.

Errors of the Doctrine…Because the existence of this doctrine depends to a great extent on the existence of "predestination," errors of the two doctrines could be interchanged. However, as we specifically consider the Calvinistic concept of "irresistible grace," many errors are glaringly evident. They are:1.) Negates the importance of man's obedience. This doctrine would have people believe that the grace of God to salvation is given to the obedient and disobedient alike, provided they have been elected.

According to Calvinism, God, in his own time, arbitrarily sends the Spirit upon whomsoever He will, while totally disregarding (a) the kind of lives these people live, and (b) the desire (or lack of it) that these people have for his grace.

Such a doctrine can only do one thing: consign obedience to the realm of the "non-essential." And when Calvinism does this, it is in complete contradiction with the Bible.

The Bible teaches that man's obedience is essential to his salvation. Jesus stated: "Not everyone that saith unto me, Lord, Lord, shall enter into the kingdom of heaven; but he that does the will of my Father which is in heaven." (Matt. 7:21)

When the Bible teaches the essentiality of obedience, it does not imply that man's obedience earns salvation. On the contrary, our active obedience to God's will indicates that we cannot save ourselves, and thus makes us openly admit that we must submit to him to be saved. Of course, this would not be the case if we were to try to be saved by obeying our will.

We read in Acts 10:34-35: "Then Peter opened his mouth, and said, of a truth I perceive that God is no respecter of persons: but in every nation he that fears him, and works righteousness, is accepted with him." Paul states the case well by contrasting the works of God with the works of man in Eph. 2:8-10 (notice the intensive words emphasis mine) , "For by grace are ye saved through faith; and that not of yourselves: it is the gift of God; not of works, lest any man should boast. For we are his workmanship, created in Christ Jesus unto good works, which God hath before ordained that we should walk in them."

Neither does the Bible imply that man's obedience displaces God's grace. The Bible teaches that God's grace, coupled with man's obedience, produces the promised blessing. This Bible principle is illustrated several times in Heb. 11.

- "By faith Noah, being warned of God of things not seen as yet (grace), moved with fear, prepared an ark (obedience) to the saving of his house (promised blessing)"
- (v. 7); "By faith Abraham, when he was called to go out into a place (grace), which he should after receive for an inheritance (promised blessing), obeyed (obedience)"
- (v. 8); "Through faith also Sara herself received strength to conceive seed (grace), and was delivered of a child when she was past age (promised blessing), because she judged him faithful who had promised (obedience)."
- (v. 11) This same principle is true today, as is shown by the statement found in Heb. 5:9: "He became the author of eternal salvation unto all them that obey him." "Eternal salvation" is the promised blessing.

Through the grace of God, Jesus shed his blood ("became the author"), which purchased the church and put into effect God's will. Man's obedience, though, must be coupled to God's grace, as is shown in the last clause: "unto all them that obey him." Hence, if obedience is essential to salvation, "irresistible grace" cannot be possible.

(2) Denies the true nature of grace. Paul explained the nature of grace in Eph. 2:8, "For by grace are ye saved through faith; and that not of yourselves: it is the gift of' God." Grace is a gift. A gift necessarily involves two ideas: (a) the will of the giver to give; and (b) the consent of the receiver to receive. If either of these conditions is missing, the item given is not a gift.

The word "irresistible" means "impossible to successfully resist" (Webster). Therefore, to state that God's grace is "irresistible" is to said that the "consent of the receiver" is not necessarily involved in the giving of grace. Hence, this would deny that the grace of God is a gift. Such is the sad consequence of believing Calvinistic theory!

(3) Destroys the free agency of man. One of the great truths of the Bible is that man is a free moral agent. He has enough intelligence to determine his course of action. God said in Deut. 30:15-18: "See, I have set before thee this day life and good, and death and evil; in ..that I command thee this day to love the Lord thy God, to walk in his ways, and to keep his commandments and his statutes and his judgments, that thou may live and multiply: and the Lord thy God shall bless thee in the land whither thou goes to possess it. But if thine heart turn away, so that thou wilt not hear, but shall be drawn away, and worship other gods, and serve them; I denounce unto you this day, that ye shall surely perish." This was true of Adam and Eve in the very beginning. They were given intelligent minds which were capable of making decisions. Two ways were set before them-the way of right and the way of wrong. God coaxed them to go the way of right and warned them against going the way of wrong-but the final decision was made by Adam and Eve.

Therefore, when man decided to go the way of wrong, he was held accountable for it. The same is true today. Jesus said, "If a man abide not in me, he is cast forth as a branch, and is withered; and men gather them and cast them into the fire, and they are burned. If ye abide in me, and my words abide in you, he shall ask what ye will and it shall be done unto you." (Jn. 15:6-7)

The vine is provided by the grace of God. But we, as branches, exercise free determination in choosing whether to abide in this vine'. Calvinism denies this. This theory would have us to believe that the elect must receive the grace of God-they have no choice about the matter. God's grace is irresistible! God certainly could not hold unsaved individuals accountable if their condition was in no way due to their own free choice. Such a theory! -it denies the most evident truths of the Bible!

It is sad but true that the grace of God can be resisted -many millions resist his grace every day. God's power to save our souls is his word (Rom. 1: 16; Jas. 1:21). When men spurn this word for their divisive human creeds, they are most surely resisting the grace of the Almighty!

Truth Magazine, XVIII:32, p. 9-10 June 13, 1974 Posted by Mark Mayberry May 3, 2012

CHAPTER FIVE:
THE SOVEREIGNTY OF GOD AND PERSEVERANCE OF THE SAINTS

Excerpts from Theopedia.com

Perseverance of the saints is the Calvinist doctrine that those who are truly saved will persevere to the end and cannot lose their salvation. It does not mean that a person who is truly saved will never lose faith or backslide at any time. But that they will ultimately persevere in faith (in spite of failures) such as not to lose their salvation.

The doctrine of perseverance is rooted in God's unconditional election and predestination. That is, since God is the One who chose and predestined the elect to salvation, therefore the elect will be saved. They might turn away from faith and give appearance of losing their salvation, but if they really are elect, they will repent and ultimately return to faith, because God is the One ensuring their salvation.

This doctrine is also closely related to the doctrine of justification and adoption. Because God is the One who justifies the elect, no one can bring any condemnation on them. In the same way because those who truly believe in Christ are adopted as God's sons, they cannot be condemned to eternal punishment (although subject to God's loving discipline as a Father).

See Westminster Confession of Faith, Chapter 17.

HISTORY OF THE DOCTRINE

The traditional doctrine is one of the five points of Calvinism that were defined at the Synod of Dort (1618-1619) during the controversy over Arminian teaching, which objected to the general predestinarian scheme of Calvinism.

The Canons of Dort (chapter 5), the Westminster Confession of Faith (Chapter XVII), and the London Baptist Confession of 1689 (Chapter 17) also include the doctrine of perseverance among other Reformed Confessions.

ETERNAL SECURITY

"Eternal security" is often seen as synonymous with "Perseverance of the saints." That is, a person who truly trusts in Christ may have assurance of eternal life with God, and thus be eternally secure. Historically, this comes from a biblical, Calvinistic framework, wherein salvation is secure because the perseverance of the saved person is certain.

Today, however, the doctrine of eternal security is usually expressed without the reference to the perseverance (or continuance) and other means of grace indicative of true saving/justifying faith. This mind-set goes hand-in-hand with the "easy believism" and "carnal Christianity" so prevalent in the evangelical church today. It is characterized by the trite phrase "once saved, always saved", suggested that one may continued in a life of willful sin and be confident of salvation because he has made a profession of faith in the past. This goes against biblical exhortations, warnings for final salvation and qualifications of true saving faith. For example:

- John 15:6 "If anyone does not abide in Me, he is thrown away as a branch and dries up; and they gather them, and cast them into the fire and they are burned."

- Heb 12:14 "Pursue peace with all men, and the sanctification without which no one will see the Lord."

- Eph 5:5-6 "For this you know with certainty, that no immoral or impure person or covetous man, who is an idolater, has an inheritance in the kingdom of Christ and God. Let no one deceive you with empty words, for because of these things the wrath of God comes upon the sons of disobedience."

- 1 John 2:3-4 "By this we know that we have come to know him, if we keep his commandments. The one who says, "I have come to know him," and does not keep his commandments, is a liar, and the truth is not in him;"

- 1 Cor. 10:1-6 "For I do not want you to be unaware, brethren, that our fathers were all under the cloud and all passed through the sea; and all were baptized into Moses in the cloud and in the sea; and all ate the same spiritual food; and all drank the same spiritual drink, for they were drinking from a spiritual rock which followed them; and the rock was Christ. Nevertheless, with most of them God was not well-pleased; for they were laid low in the wilderness."

- 2 Cor 13:5 "Test yourselves {to see} if you are in the faith; examine yourselves! Or do you not recognize this about yourselves, that Jesus Christ is in you--unless indeed you fail the test?

If we persevere to gain salvation, we have missed the truth of the gospel message. A Christian will preserve because he loves the Lord and seeks to walk with Jesus in this world. This has nothing to do with eternal security or predestination. There are other scriptures that teach eternal security and predestination that are not Calvinistic. Here are a few:

"For ye have not received the spirit of bondage again to fear; but ye have received the Spirit of adoption, whereby we cry, Abba, Father. The Spirit itself bears witness with our spirit, that we are the children of God" Romans 8:15-16.

"These things have I written unto you that believe on the name of the

Son of God; that ye may know that ye have eternal life, and that ye may believe on the name of the Son of God." I John 5:13.

"And we know that all things work together for good to them that love God, to them who are the called according to *his* purpose. For whom he did foreknow, he also did predestinate *to be* conformed to the image of his Son, that he might be the firstborn among many brethren. Moreover whom he did predestinate, them he also called: and whom he called, them he also justified: and whom he justified, them he also glorified." Romans8-30.

Note: The predestination in v-30 of Romans, chapter eight, is actually a destination which is to be conformed to the image of his Son, Jesus. It referees to God's will for those who, in his foreknowledge, he knew would believe. There is no arbitrary pre-selection of some with the rest damned. It has nothing to do with eternal security or even salvation, although they are implied. It is all about image and character. The destination is to be Christ-like.

It also reveals the selection process of the elect is based upon his foreknowledge as is his calling. It is not based on any other choice that may be unknown to us now. His selection and calling and his justification are all based on his ability to see the future. He knew ahead of time who would respond to his call and who would not.

We should dismiss critical arguments that say, if God had to look down through history to determine who would be his children, he would not be all knowing. That is foolishness. The fact that God is all powerful, knowing all, says he would possess foreknowledge. Because he is all knowing, he would, of course, know ahead of time all things, not just who would come to Christ.

God chose us to be Christ-like. God made this choice so that Jesus would be the firstborn of many brethren. V-30 The choice was made before the beginning and was based on his own foreknowledge. Then he called us to himself, justified us by the death of Jesus and his resurrection. He then glorified us with his presence.

It is important to see that man is not sovereign. He is rarely in control of the events that shape his life. However, God has still given man free will to choose his lifestyle. In effect, we can be evil, nice, straight, gay or be and do anything we want. Our choices, however, come with consequences.

"Be not deceived; God is not mocked: for whatsoever a man soweth, that shall he also reap." (Gal. 6:7)

Jonathan Edwards, a 17th century Christian preacher and theologian, said that the will is the mind choosing: though there is a distinction between mind and will, the two are inseparable in action. We do not make a choice without our mind's approving that choice. We choose according to our strongest inclination at a given moment.

Edwards taught that man was not free to choose God because it is contrary to my nature. That is why we need new natures that are given to us by the Holy Spirit at regeneration.

Unless a man is "Born Again" he cannot enter or even see the kingdom of God. (John 3).

He felt that man is commanded to seek the Lord while he may be found, and to come to Christ, but we watch in vain for man to do so. Romans 3:11 literally reads,

"There is no God seeker."

John 6:44 said, *"No one can come to Me, (Jesus), unless the Father who sent Me draws him and I will raise him up on the last day."*

Literally, the verse said, "no one is able." (This is the calling of the elect. It is by God the Father. It proves that salvation is started by God, not man.)

Edwards was a Calvinists preacher. He did not agree with "universal election."

Gerhard Kittel's Theological Dictionary of the New Testament says that the word translated draw in John 6:44 means "to compel by irresistible authority."

"Draw" was used in classical Greek for drawing water from a well. We do not entice or persuade water to leave the well; we force it against gravity to come up by drawing it. So it is with us. We are so depraved that God must drag us to himself." (Chosen by God)

The controversy is in whom God has chosen to be his sons and daughters. Hyper-Calvinists believe that some are chosen and some are not from the foundation of the world.

Arminians believe God choose those who he knew would come to him. They believe in "Total Depravity" but also the ability of God to speak to the dead and call them forth for his glory.

Judas, the one who betrayed him, had betrayed himself and met his just due. John wrote, ". Jesus knew from the beginning...who should betray him. And he said, ... no man can come unto me, except it were given unto him of my Father ... Have not I chosen you twelve, and one of you is a devil (i.e., slanderer) ... He spoke of Judas ... for he it was that should betray him, being one of the twelve." (John 6:64-71.) Our God cannot fail, lie, or sin. Neither is he frustrated at man's failure.

God is the author of his sovereign grace and mercy. "For he saith to Moses, I will have mercy on whom I will have mercy, and I will have compassion on whom I will have compassion. So, it is not of him that wills, nor of him that runs, but of God that shows mercy... And whom he will, he hardened." (Rom. 9:15-16, 18.)

Many Christians have doubts about God's sovereignty. Yet there is one aspect of the Christian life where they profess, maybe unknowingly, that God is sovereign. They may said, as many do, "God has done all he can do, now the rest is up to you."

How contradictory! They may stand on their feet and deny this blessed, comforting, enabling doctrine, but when they bend their knees in prayer, asking God to save them, do they not realize they are calling on a sovereign God, who only he has the right and the ability to save? The question is, If God has done all that he can do, why pray to him? But we pray knowing he is the only one who can do what man cannot otherwise do. This power belongs to God, and not man. (Excerpts from Sovereign Grace Baptist Proclaimer)

CHAPTER SIX:
THE SOVEREIGNTY OF GOD AND ARMINIAN THEOLOGY

The Arminians were people of Armenia that began as a group in the 6th century. The earliest religious beliefs of Arminians are believed to have been a blend of Indo-European, Mesopotamian, and native Anatolian beliefs.

Christianity spread into the country as early as AD 40. Tiridates III of Armenia (238–314) made Christianity the state religion in 301, ten years before the Roman Empire granted Christianity an official toleration under Galerius, and 36 years before Constantine the Great was baptized. Prior to this, during the latter part of the Parthian period.

Arminians can legitimately claim a historical continuity of some 4000 years; their history is among those of the most ancient peoples in the world.

WHAT IS ARMINIANISM?

(Excerpts from Biblereanson.com)

Jacob Arminius was a 16th century Dutch theologian who originally was a student of John Calvin before changing his beliefs. Some of his beliefs that were changed included his understanding of Soteriology (the Doctrine of Salvation.)

While Calvinism emphasizes God's sovereignty, Arminianism places the emphasis on man's responsibility and claims that he has a completely free will.

Jacob Arminius was ordained in 1588. The latter part of his life became full of controversy for which he would be known throughout history. During a season of his life when he was called to bring charges of heresy against a man, he began to question his understanding of the doctrine of predestination, which led him to question his stances on the nature and character of God. He thought predestination was too harsh for a loving God. He began to promote a "conditional election" that allowed both man and God to take part in the salvation process.

After his death, his followers would promote his teachings. They perpetuated his views by authorizing and signing the Remonstrance. In 1610 the Remonstrant Arminianism was debated at the Synod of Dort, which was the official gathering of the Dutch Reformed Church. Delegates from England, Germany, Switzerland and the Dutch Church were present, and all voted in favor of Gomarus (who promoted the historic Augustinianism view.) The Arminians were dismissed, and many persecuted. However, five theological points came from their presentation that changed the Christin world.

THE FIVE POINTS OF ARMINIANISM

1. **Human Free Will ...**This is also referred to as Partial Depravity. This belief states that man is depraved due to the fall, but man is still able to come to God and accept salvation. Arminians claim that people, despite their fallen state, can still make a spiritually good decision to follow Christ based on the grace that God gives to all people.

Verses Used By Arminians To Support This:

John 3:16-17 "For God so loved the world that he gave his only begotten Son, that whoever believes in him should not perish but have everlasting life. For God did not send his Son into the world to condemn the world, but that the world through him might be saved."

John 3:36 "He who believes in the Son has everlasting life; and he who does not believe the Son shall not see life, but the wrath of God abides on him."

2. Conditional Election

Conditional election states that God only "chooses" those whom he knows will choose to believe. This belief says that God looks down the long hallway of time into the future to see who is going to choose him.

 Verses Arminians use to support conditional election.

Jeremiah 1:5 "Before I formed you in the womb, I knew you; before you were born, I sanctified you; I ordained you a prophet to the nations."

Romans 8:29 "For whom He foreknew, He also predestined."

3. Universal Atonement

Also known as Unlimited Atonement. This belief says that Jesus's death on the cross was for all of humanity and that anyone can be saved simply by believing in him. This belief states that Christ's redeeming work made it possible for everyone to be saved, but that it did not actually secure salvation for anyone.

 Verses Arminians use to support universal atonement

1 John 2:2 "He is the propitiation for our sins, and not for ours only, but also for the sins of the whole world."

John 1:29 "The next day he saw Jesus coming toward him, and said, 'Behold, the Lamb of God, who takes away the sins of the world!"

Titus 2:11 "For the grace of God has appeared, bringing salvation for all people."

4. Resistible Grace

This teaching emphasizes that individuals can resist the grace of God until it is completely extinguished. This teaching says that God inwardly calls people who are also called outwardly, that God does all he can to bring a sinner to salvation – but man can thwart that calling and harden himself to God.

Verses Arminians use to support resistible grace.

Hebrews 3:15 "While it is aid, 'Today if you will hear his voice, do not harden your hearts as in the rebellion."

1 Thessalonians 5:19 "Do not quench the Spirit."

5. **Fall from Grace**

This is the Arminian teaching that claims that a person can become saved, and then lose his salvation. This happens when a person fails to keep up their faith or commits a grievous sin. But how many sins? or how many times we must fail to have perfect faith? It's all a bit cloudy. Arminians are not entirely agreed upon this doctrinal stance.

Verses Arminians use to support fall from grace.

Galatians 5:4 "You have become estranged from Christ, you who attempt to be justified by law; you have fallen from grace."

Hebrews 6:4-6 "For it is impossible for those who were once enlightened, and have tasted the heavenly gift, and have become partakers of the Holy Spirit, and have tasted the good word of God and the powers of the age to come, if they fall away, to renew them again to repentance, since they crucify again for themselves the Son of God, and put him to an open shame."

I want to discuss this point in more detail because I believe you cannot fall from God's grace once you have been, "Born Again" Here is my scriptural evaluation.

God chooses, redeems, and seals everyone who is saved forever. Since salvation was not because of anything that we do ourselves – we cannot be the cause of it failing.

Our salvation is eternally an act of God's power and sovereignty over his creation – an act that is totally for his glory. Galatians 5:4 does not teach that you can lose your salvation. This verse frightens many people when it is read out of context. In this book, Paul had already been addressing those people who were trying to add to faith by including works-based salvation in the act of circumcision. These were the Judaizers. They were not denying faith in Christ, nor were they requiring all the law be kept – they were requiring a bit of both.

Paul argues against their inconsistency and explains that we cannot go down both paths. Paul is saying that they were still seeking their justification. They were not like the true believers who professed faith in Christ, alone (Romans 5:1.) They were estranged from Christ, not in the fact that they had ever been united with Christ in salvation – but they were estranged from the only true source of eternal life – Christ alone. They had fallen from the grace alone doctrine and were destroying that concept by their beliefs of adding works to it.

Hebrews 6 is another passage that often worries individuals. We must look at it in context – especially since it starts with the word "therefore." We need to see what the "therefore" is there for. Here the author is explaining that Jesus is better than the priests or the temple – even better than Melchizedek. He explains that all the Old Testament law was pointing towards Jesus, that Jesus is the completion of it.

This passage in Hebrews 6 says that these people were enlightened. The word enlightened is not used in scripture to indicate someone who has been saved. They were knowledgeable. It does not say anywhere that they believed. They were curious. They got a little sampling of Christianity. These people were never saved to begin with. Hebrews 6 is not talking about losing your salvation.

1 Thessalonians 5:23-24 "Now may the God of peace himself sanctify you entirely; and may your spirit and soul and body be preserved complete,

without blame at the coming of our Lord Jesus Christ. Faithful is he who calls you, and he also will bring it to pass."

1 John 2:19 "They went out from us, but they were not really of us; for if they had been of us, they would have remained with us; but they went out, so that it would be shown that they all are not of us."

FAMOUS ARMINIAN PREACHERS AND THEOLOGIANS

Jacob Arminius, John Wesley, Charles Wesley, Andrew Murray, R. A. Torrey, David Wilkerson, John R. Rice

Now that you have a clearer understanding of both Arminianism and the Sovereignty of God, according to John Calvan, let us talk about the "Free Will" of man.

Pastor Steve Weaver, Hamburg Bible Church, writes, "A good definition of free will is the ability of the mind to make choices in accordance with our natures."

This definition of "free will" also applies to God's free will. He, too, is bound by his divine nature. Therefore, he cannot sin! Why? Because it is not his nature! But God does have a free will and, unlike human beings, he has an accompanying good and holy nature.

Jonathan Edwards, a 17th-century Christian preacher and theologian, said that the will is the mind choosing: (though there is a distinction between mind and will, the two are inseparable in action.) We do not choose without our minds approving that choice. We choose according to our strongest inclination at any moment.

The Bible teaches that I am not free to choose God because it is contrary to my nature. That is why we need new natures that are given to us by the Holy Spirit at regeneration. Unless a man is "Born Again" he cannot enter or even see the kingdom of God (John 3).

Though man is commanded to seek the Lord while he may be found, and to come to Christ, we watch in vain for man to do so. Romans 3:11 literally reads, "There is no God seeker." John 6:44 said, "No one can come to me, (Jesus), unless the Father who sent me draws him and I will raise him on the last day." The verse said, "No one is able." This is "Total Depravity".

Gerhard Kittel's Theological Dictionary of the New Testament said that the word translated as *draw* in John 6:44 means "to compel by irresistible authority." In classical Greek, they used it for drawing water from a well. We do not entice or persuade water to leave the well; we force it against gravity to come up by drawing it. So it is with us. We are so depraved that God must drag us to himself." (Chosen by God. (This is the Calvinistic belief. It is not mine)

The controversy is about whom God has chosen to be his sons and daughters. Hyper-Calvinists believe God chooses some people and does not choose others from the foundation of the world. "Free Will" folks, *of which I am one*, believe that what Jesus said, as recorded in John 3:16, qualifies all that accept his invitation. Listen to the verse and pay particular attention to the word "WHOSOEVER"

"For God so loved the world that he gave his only begotten Son, that **whosoever** believeth in him should not perish, but have everlasting life." John 3:16.

Jesus died for the sins of the entire world...every man, woman, boy, and girl. The compelling call of God, through Jesus, is an open invitation. God chooses these individuals, pulling them out of sin and giving them a new heart capable of believing and worshiping him. (Total depravity cannot stop the call of God to the spiritually dead. They can hear and respond.)

Those that God chose before the foundation of the world, called, justified, and glorified, are the "Whosoever" generation that is being gathered even now from every generation since Adam until the return of Christ.

CHAPTER SEVEN: THE SOVEREIGNTY OF GOD AND FOREKNOWLEDGE

Now let us look at how free will and sovereignty work hand and hand in our daily lives to fulfill God's master plan for the ages. Miles Monroe, a famous evangelist, once explained it this way...when God created all that there is; he drew up a master plan, like an architect. In his master plan, he considered every soul and every action that man would take. Nothing was left out.

God is never taken by surprise because he saw it before the world was. He incorporated it into his plan. Then he created, taking into account who would accept Jesus and who would not; who would need deliverance; who would need help, etc. Every prayer and every need were seen beforehand. Your provision was made way back then and is waiting for the time that you need it. You just need to grab it by faith.

This pre-design gives us free will to choose without violating God's sovereignty. I know that some will say, I prayed and believed but did not get what I asked for. My provision did not materialize. It could be as James 4:3 said, "Ye ask, and receive not, because ye ask amiss, that ye may consume it upon your lusts." David Wilkerson, the author of The Cross & The Switchblade, offers six reasons that prayers go unanswered.

- Our Prayers Are Aborted When They Are Not According To God's Will.

- Our Prayers Can Be Aborted When They Are Designed To Fulfill An Inner Lust, Dreams, Or Illusions.

- Our Prayers Can Be Denied When We Show No Diligence to Assist God In The Answer.

- Our Prayers Can Be Aborted By A Secret Grudge Lodged In the Heart Against Another.

- Our Prayers Can Be Aborted By Not Expecting Much To Come of Them.

- Our Prayers Are Aborted When We Attempt To Prescribe How God Should Answer.

See his full explanation at http://www.tscpulpitseries.org/english/undated/tssixrea.html

The devil's final strategy in deceiving believers is to make them doubt the faithfulness of God in answering prayer. Satan would have us believe God has shut his ears to our cry and left us to work things out for ourselves. That is just not true. If you do not see the hand of God, you can bet that the problem is with you, not God. I would suggest that you go back before the throne of God and stay there until you get an answer. Don't forget to take your Bible with you. *"Let us therefore come boldly unto the throne of grace that we may obtain mercy, and find grace to help in time of need."* (Hebrews 4:16)

One final thought. You may not be hearing the Lord because you are not "Born Again." Listen to what Jesus said, John 10:26-27, "But you do not believe because you are not part of my flock. My sheep hear my voice, and I know them, and they follow me." If you are not hearing his voice, well, what should I say? You are not of his flock? Only you can determine that. It is a total life-changing commitment to follow Jesus. Maybe you did not make that kind of commitment. He must be Lord of all or he is not Lord at all.

Foreknowledge does not take away from God's sovereignty. Some critics of free will argue that if God had to look down the halls of time to see who would be saved, it implies that he is not all-knowing. This argument is foolish because God is all- knowing and because he is all-knowing, he knew who would accept his invitation to be saved. He did not have to look anywhere to discover that. He knew because he is God.

Foreknowledge, in biblical contexts, refers to **God's omniscience**, meaning His complete knowledge and understanding of all things. It encompasses not only past and present events but also future occurrences. God's foreknowledge is a central characteristic of his divine nature, highlighting his sovereignty and wisdom. It is the state of knowing everything:

1. Definition

Foreknowledge is God's knowledge of events that, from the human point of view, are the future. It constitutes his prescience—the ability to know what will happen before it occurs.

God is represented as having knowledge of the entire course of events before they take place. Such knowledge belongs to the Scriptural idea of God from the very outset of special revelation.

2. Biblical Basis:

In the Old Testament, God's foreknowledge is often expressed using the Hebrew verb yada (יָדַע), which means "to know." This verb signifies God's awareness of future events.

In the New Testament, the main verbs associated with foreknowledge are proginosko (προγινώσκω), meaning what is ahead. foreknowledge closely connects to concepts like election and predestination, as well as to God's sovereign rule over the universe.

3. Examples:

God's Knowledge of Individuals:

- Psalm 139:16 states, "the days ordained for me were written in your book before one of them came to be." God knows our thoughts, words, and life's work even before our birth.

- Jeremiah was set apart in the womb to be a prophet (Jeremiah 1:5).

- God's choice of Abraham and Israel demonstrates his foreknowledge (Genesis 18:19; Amos 3:2a; Romans 11:2.

Specific Prophecies:

Old Testament

- Micaiah predicted Ahab's death (1 Kings 22:17).

- Isaiah anticipated the coming of Cyrus (Isaiah 41:2; 44:28; 45:1).

- Micah prophesied the Messiah's birth in Bethlehem (Micah 5:2).

- God can work through evil actions to accomplish His purposes (e.g., Joseph's brothers selling him as a slave, leading to salvation for many; Genesis 45:5-7).

New Testament:

- Christ, chosen as the Redeemer before the creation of the world, exemplifies God's foreknowledge (1 Peter 1:20).

- God's foreknowledge is linked to Christ's death and the salvation of the elect.

In summary, God's foreknowledge transcends time, encompassing all events—past, present, and future—while emphasizing his sovereignty and wisdom.

CHAPTER EIGHT:
THE SOVEREIGNTY OF GOD AND DIVINE GRACE

What is grace? The Bible dictionary says it is "Unmerited Favor" Another word for unmerited is undeserved. It also denotes a sense of guilt as in committing an offense or lawlessness act. When we come to Biblical evaluations, we can easily see how man has broken God's law and is thus guilty before the court of God's final justice.

I know what you are saying. You don't hurt anyone. You try to be good, but no one is perfect. You're doing pretty good in a world of imperfect folks. There are a lot of other folks that do worse things than you. That may be fine, but measuring yourself by the actions of others cannot set you free from your own sin. The only thing that can save you from yourself is the mercy of God. When you finally recognize that you are guilty before a just and holy God, who, by the way, created you, you will plead for his mercy. You have come face to face with the sovereignty of God. It is your opinion against his holy decree. You may not know that God is always right. That's what sovereignty is all about. He is the Supreme ruler of all things, including you. He declares you are guilty and must face punishment for your sin.

The problem is, he is righteous, perfect is every way and you are not. Do you want to know why you fall short of his perfection? Read Romans 5:12. Here's what it says:

"Wherefore, as by one man sin entered into the world, and death by sin;

and so, death passed upon all men, for that all have sinned:" Romans 5:12.

People commonly know this event as the fall of man. It started with Adam's sin against God and his loss of God's image. He became a walking dead man. All his descendants were born with that same sinful nature. They could not attain the spiritual union with God as Adam once had. They were bound by a sinful nature that pulled them into darkness.

So, man now looks towards the only hope he has of eternal life outside of hell. His call is, "Be merciful unto me, oh Lord, for I have sinned." He calls upon the mercy of God, knowing that God is sovereign but also merciful.

Why should God be merciful to sinners? Jesus answered this question as recorded by John, the apostle." For God so LOVED the world, that he gave his only begotten Son, that whosoever believes on him shall have eternal life." John 3:16.

The motivation for God's mercy towards man is his love. However, not just a passing love, but a perfect love. He ***So Loved*** the world, and that is why he is merciful towards it.

Bible verses about the mercy of God:

- James 2:13 - For he shall have judgment without mercy, that has shewed no mercy; and mercy rejoices against judgment.

- Luke 6:36 - Be ye therefore merciful, as your Father also is merciful.

- Matthew 5:7 - Blessed are the merciful: for they shall obtain mercy.

- Hebrews 4:16 - Let us therefore come boldly unto the throne of grace, that we may obtain mercy, and find grace to help in time of need.

- Ephesians 2:4-5 - But God, who is rich in mercy, for his great love wherewith he loved us.

Remember, we are discussing free will and the sovereignty of God. Question? Can a loving merciful God damn billions to an eternity in hell? I have already answered this question but want to restate it so you get the point.

God sends no one to hell. They end up there because of their own free will. "Enter ye in at the strait gate: for wide *is* the gate, and broad *is* the way, that leads to destruction, and many there be which go in thereat:" Matthew 7:13.

Did you notice that there is a wide road that leads to destruction and a lot of folks will go down it to their destruction? Jesus told this to his disciples, and it has stayed in force ever since. We need to be "Straight Gate" folks.

Divine grace is a theological term present in many religions. Scholars define divine grace as the divine influence that regenerates and sanctifies humans, inspires virtuous impulses, and imparts strength to endure trial and resist temptation.

Grace is a concept deeply rooted in Christian theology. It holds profound significance for believers. Let's explore some of its benefits:

Grace enables us to forgive others, just as someone has forgiven us. Following Christ's example, we extend grace to those who wrong us. By forgiving, we free ourselves from negative emotions and find happiness and peace.

Peace: Practicing grace leads to a more peaceful existence. When we love others and treat them as we wish to be treated, grudges and negativity find no place in our hearts.

Hope: Through grace, we have the hope of everlasting life. It assures us that God has plans for our future, filled with hope and purpose.

Healing: Grace makes healing possible. Christ's willingness to bear the punishment meant for us brings healing to our souls.

Justification: Grace justifies us before God. It declares us righteous despite our flaws and shortcomings.

Transformation: Grace transforms us. It empowers us to live godly lives, teaching us to honor God and bring glory to his name.

Empowerment: Grace puts us in charge. It empowers us to reign in life, overcoming challenges and adversities.

Access to God: Grace provides us access to God, allowing us to communicate and fellowship with Him.

Intimacy with God: It establishes a new relationship of intimacy with God, strengthening our faith and deepening our connection with Him.

Discipline and Training: Grace disciplines and trains us to live in a way that honors God. It shapes our character and guides our actions.

Remember, God's grace is a gift—unmerited and freely given. It is a treasure that enriches our lives and points us back to Christ's glory. (Excerpts from Copilot)

Hebrewsendurance.com offers this: According to the Blue Letter Bible, the typical usage of the word cháris was: "of the merciful kindness by which God, exerting his holy influence upon souls, turns them to Christ, keeps, strengthens, increases them in Christian faith, knowledge, affection, and kindles them to the exercise of the Christian virtues"

God's grace is not only lavished on us, but it also exerts an influence on us that draws us to Christ through whom we can be saved.

If you think about it for a second, you'll realize that everyone has been the recipient of God's grace–to one extent or another. It is because of God's grace that anyone is still alive today. The Bible says all have sinned and come short of the glory of God (Romans 3:23). There is not a single person on earth who has perfectly lived up to the will of God, except Jesus.

CHAPTER NINE:
THE SOVEREIGNTY
OF GOD AND HELL

The end of days is fast approaching and we need to be assured of our salvation and focused on those things that really count. Knowing that there is a hell and understanding how to escape it, as a destiny, is the most important thing anyone can do.

How many times have you told someone to, **"Go To Hell"?** How many times has someone told you the same thing? If we knew the type of place that hell is, we would not be telling others to go there.

Webster defines hell as "A place regarded in various religions as a spiritual realm of evil and suffering, often traditionally depicted as a place of perpetual fire beneath the earth where the wicked are punished after death."

The Bible definition goes like this: "Hell" is the future place of eternal punishment of the damned, including the devil and his fallen angels. There are several words rendered as "Hell. "

Hades--A Greek word. It is the place of the dead--the location of the person between death and resurrection. *(See Matt. 11:23, 16:18, Acts 11:27, 1 Cor.*

15:55, Rev. 1:18, 6:8).

Gehenna--A Greek word. It was the place where dead bodies were dumped and burned (2 Kings 23:13-14). Jesus used the word to designate the place of eternal torment (Matt. 5:22, 29, 30, Mark 9:43, Luke 12:5).

Sheol--A Hebrew word. It is the place of the dead and not necessarily the grave, but the place the dead go to. It is used of both the righteous (Psalm 16:10, 30:3, Isaiah 38:10) and the wicked (Num. 16:33, Job. 24:19, Psalm 9:17).

Hell... is a place of eternal fire (Matt. 25:41, Rev. 19:20). It was prepared for the devil and his angels, (Matt. 25:41) and will be the abode of the wicked (Rev. 21:8) and the fallen angels (2 Pet. 2:4)."

It's not a place where the average folks would want to go, visit or live. But, according to Jesus, many will go there. "Enter ye in at the strait gate: for wide *is* the gate, and broad *is* the way, that leads to destruction, and many there be which go in thereat:" Matthew 7:13

THE HORROR OF HELL

Tom Ascol of Ligonier Ministries shares four truths about hell that Jesus taught in Matthew 25:41-46. These truths should cause us to grieve over the prospect of anyone experiencing its horrors.

First, hell is a state of separation from God. On the day of judgment, Jesus will said to all unbelievers, "Depart from me, you cursed, into the eternal fire" (v. 41). This is the same sort of language that Jesus uses elsewhere to describe the final judgment of unbelievers (see 7:23).

To be separated from God is to be separated from anything and everything good. That is hard to understand because even the most miserable person enjoys some of God's blessings. We breathe his air, are nourished by food that he supplies, and experience many other aspects of his common grace.

On earth, even atheists enjoy the benefits of God's goodness. But in hell, these blessings will be nonexistent. Those consigned there will remember God's goodness, and will even have some awareness of the unending pleasures of heaven, but they will have no access to them.

This does not mean that God will be completely absent from hell. He is and will remain omnipresent (Ps. 139:7–8). To be separated from the Lord and cast into hell does not mean that a person will finally be free of God. That person will remain eternally accountable to him. He will remain Lord over the person's existence. But in hell, a person will experience eternal separation from God's kindness, mercy, grace, and goodness. He will assign him to face his holy wrath.

Second, hell is a state of association. Jesus said that the eternal fire of hell was "prepared for the devil and his angels" (Matt. 25:41). God made people for Himself. God made hell for the devil. Yet people who die in their sin, without Jesus Christ as Lord and Savior, will spend eternity in hell with the one being who is most unlike God. It is a tragic irony that many who do not believe in the devil in this life will wind up spending eternity being tormented with him in hell.

Third, hell is a state of punishment. Jesus describes it as "fire" (v. 41) and a place of "punishment" (v. 46). Hell is a place of retribution where justice is served through the payment for crimes.

The punishment must fit the crime. The misery and torment of hell points to the wickedness and seriousness of sin. Those who protest the Biblical doctrine of hell as being excessive betray their inadequate comprehension of the sinfulness of sin. For sinners to be consigned to anything less than the horrors of eternal punishment would be a miscarriage of justice.

Finally, the fourth truth is that hell is an everlasting state. Though some would like to shorten the duration of this state, Jesus' words are very clear. He uses the same adjective to describe both punishment and life in verse 46. If hell is not eternal, neither is the new heaven and earth.

How can God exact infinite punishment for a finite sin?

Because the person against whom all sin is committed is infinite. Crimes against the infinitely holy, infinitely kind, infinitely good, and infinitely supreme Ruler of the world deserve unending punishment. Besides that, those condemned to hell will go on sinning for eternity. There is no repentance in hell. So, the punishment will continue as long as the sinning does.

The dreadfulness of hell deepens our grateful praise for the salvation we have in Jesus Christ. Hell is what we deserve and hell is what he experienced on the cross in our place.

Believing the truth about hell also motivates us to persuade people to be reconciled to God. By God's grace, those of us who are trusting Christ have been rescued from this horrible destiny. How can we love people and refuse to speak plainly to them about the reality of eternal damnation and God's gracious provision of salvation? Clearer visions of hell will give us greater love for both God and people.

HOW CAN A LOVING GOD

Condemn So Many To Hell?

I have a few friends that tell me, in no uncertain terms, that they cannot understand how a loving God can damn to hell so many people. It is obvious that they do not comprehend the concept of the "Free Will" of man.

God is in full control of his creation. Part of that control is to allow man to have a free will to also be in full control. It's all a matter of sovereignty.

When you gather thousands or even a few folks together that are all exercising their free will, things can get ugly. Some will get drunk; others will kill or steal and yet others will exercise righteous judgment in life. All this interaction of free wills brings on different opinions, different lifestyles, and different attitudes.

If God intervenes to stop the flow of our "Free will" decisions, he tampers with the future and denies man his right to be a free moral agent. His actions would contradict his own will and plan for humanity. Man must be free to choose his own way to escape a robotic existence that is not what God or man wants.

However, with this gift of "Free Will" comes responsibility. The Bible says that the soul that sins will die..." Behold, all souls are mine; as the soul of the father, so also the soul of the son is mine: the soul that sins, it shall die." Ezekiel 18:4

"Be not deceived; God is not mocked: for whatsoever a man soweth, that shall he also reap." Galatians 6:7

"For all have sinned, and come short of the glory of God;" Romans 3:23.

It should be obvious by now that **God sends no one to hell**. He does, however, allow people to send themselves to hell by their own choices in life. Our life choices affect our destiny. They take us down the road to destruction or up the road to eternal life.

This concept is not new. We need only to look at a man that drinks a lot and we can conclude that if he does not slack off, he will become a drunk. We can see it coming. The same is true when we look at a person who cares not about their eternal soul, lives for today, denies the existence of God, and ignores the truths of the Bible. We can say, if he does not repent, he will ultimately end up in hell. We can see it coming.

I have already delt with those that have never heard the gospel and what happens to them in chapter five.

IS THE DEVIL IN CHARGE OF HELL?

No one takes charge of anything, but according to Revelation 20:10, they throw the devil into hell and ultimately the lake of fire. The lost will not find a party in hell. There is no reward. There is no pleasure at all.

WHERE IS HELL?

Your guess is as good as mine. People have put forward various theories on the location of hell. A traditional view is that hell is in the center of the earth. Others propose that hell is in outer space in a black hole. In the

Old Testament, the word translated "hell" is Sheol; in the New Testament, it is Hades (meaning "unseen") and Gehenna ("the Valley of Hinnom"). Sheol is also translated as "pit" and "grave." Both Sheol and Hades refer to a temporary abode of the dead before judgment (Psalm 9:17; Revelation 1:18). Gehenna refers to an eternal state of punishment for the wicked dead (Mark 9:43).

In the King James Version, Ephesians 4:9 said that before Jesus ascended into heaven, "he also descended.... into the lower parts of the earth." Some Christians take "the lower parts of the earth" as a reference to hell, where they said Jesus spent the time between his death and resurrection. However, the New International Version gives a better translation: "he also descended to the lower, earthly regions." This verse simply says that Jesus came to earth. It is a reference to his incarnation, not to his location after death.

The notion that hell is somewhere in outer space, possibly in a black hole, is based on the knowledge that black holes are places of great heat and pressure from which nothing, not even light, can escape. Surprisingly, the 1979 Walt Disney film The Black Hole presents this concept of hell.

Another speculation is that the earth itself will be the "lake of fire" spoken of in Revelation 20:10-15. When the earth is destroyed by fire (2 Peter 3:10; Revelation 21:1), as the theory goes, God will use that burning sphere as the everlasting place of torment for the ungodly. Again, this is mere speculation.

To sum up, Scripture does not tell us the geological (or cosmological) location of hell. Hell is a literal place of real torment, but we do not know where it is. Hell may have a physical location in this universe, or it may be in an entirely different "dimension." Whatever the case, the location of hell is far less important than the need to avoid going there.

WHAT IS HELL REALLY LIKE?

The Bible tells us that God is light and that there is no darkness in him.

When a soul is separated from God, there is no light, only total darkness. There are no friendships, only total isolation...all alone forever. It is a place of torment. I believe that the ultimate torment is to see God, feel his love and splendor and must live with the fact that you can never have it.

I also see the deep cravings of the flesh being manifested, but never fulfilled. Then there is the fire and stench of burning flesh. This type of fire cannot be quenched. It will burn with the wrath of God forever.

I realize that this is a morbid picture and a horrible destiny but that is what Jesus said, "There shall be weeping and gnashing of teeth, when ye shall see Abraham, and Isaac, and Jacob, and all the prophets, in the kingdom of God, and you yourselves thrust out". Luke 13:28.

THE CONTROVERSY OVER ETERNAL SUFFERING OF THE WICKED AND THEIR ANNIHILATION

There is a controversy over eternal suffering and annihilation. Some folks believe that the souls in hell suffer forever. Others read "And death and hell were cast into the lake of fire. This is the second death." Revelation 20:14 and conclude that this 2nd death is total annihilation.

The premise for this conclusion is, "And God shall wipe away all tears from their eyes; and there shall be no more death, neither sorrow, nor crying, neither shall there be any more pain: for the former things are passed away." Revelation 21:14.

The thought is that our tears are caused by knowing some of our loved ones are suffering in hell and the fact that we remember them no more is because of the end of their suffering by the 2nd death. As hopeful as this thought process is, it is not Biblical because it goes against what God has spoken about the wicked and their destiny.

Many folks that do not believe in God, said, "Even if there is a God and he sends me to hell, it's not forever". "I will end up non-existent, as though I never existed...so, that justifies my so-called sin now, to eat, drink and be merry." Without an absolute penalty, there is no fear of judgment because the punishment is temporary.

When God wipes away all our tears, I believe he removes the memory of all the bad stuff, including those that chose against God and ended up in eternal damnation.

ARE PEOPLE SUFFERING IN HELL RIGHT NOW?

Jesus related a story about a rich man and a beggar. Here is what he said as recorded by Luke 16:20-24.

"And there was a certain beggar named Lazarus, which was laid at his gate, full of sores and desiring to be fed with the crumbs, which fell from the rich man's table: moreover, the dogs came and licked his sores.

And it came to pass that the beggar died, and was carried by the angels into Abraham's bosom: the rich man also died, and was buried; **And in hell he lifted his eyes, being in torment** and sees Abraham afar off, and Lazarus in his bosom.

And he cried and said, Father Abraham, have mercy on me, and send Lazarus, that he may dip the tip of his finger in water, and cool my tongue; for I am tormented in this flame.

I realize that this was just a story that Jesus related. However, there are several important points to consider:

The wicked die and find themselves in hell in torment. It is an immediate happening. It is therefore a picture of reality. The Bible also confirms this, "And as it is appointed unto men once to die, but after this the judgment" Hebrews 9:27.

- The torment was hell fire.
- The suffering was of the body and soul.

- Those assigned to hell cannot leave.
- They have no way to quench the flames or find any sort of comfort.

They could hear, thirst, feel pain and sorrow, and even communicate with those in paradise. But the one thing that the people in hell could not do was to cease to exist.

After the resurrection of Christ, things concerning hell changed. Jesus went to hell, took the keys of hell and death (Rev. 1:18), and set the captives free—those who were in Abraham's bosom.

Ephesians 4: 9-10 says,

"Now that he ascended, what is it but that he also descended first into the lower parts of the earth? He that descended is the same also that ascended far above all heavens, that he might fill all things."

After defeating the devil and setting the captives free, Jesus took those in Abraham's bosom to heaven with him, where all believers go now. But we will not live in heaven forever. We only live in heaven until the end of the age. Then God is going to make a new heaven and a new earth, and all the believers will live there with Jesus in the new Jerusalem which is on the new earth. (Rev. 21:1-4)

When you die in your sins, you go straight to hell. You do not pass go or collect $200. The game is over and you lost big-time. You experience death physically, torment until the end of all things and then a 2nd death of your eternal soul as it is cast into the lake of fire. Your suffering will last forever.

"And fear not them which kill the body, but are not able to kill the soul: but rather fear him which is able to destroy both soul and body in hell." Matthew 10:28

Although it was never intended for man, hell is an awful place where those who reject so great a sacrifice will join the devil and his angels for eternity. (Rev. 20:10)

THE UNPARDONABLE SIN

The Bible makes it clear that the Holy Spirit convicts us of sin, and there is only one sin that can send us to hell. That is the sin of rejecting the sacrifice of Jesus Christ.

"And when he (the Holy Spirit) is come, he will reprove the world of sin (singular), and of righteousness, and of judgment: of sin, because they believe not on me." (John 16: 8-) Excerpts taken from Andrew Womack Ministries article "Hell, A Reality or Metaphor?"

THE FINAL PUNISHMENT OF THE WICKED

There is a punishment for sinners who refuse to repent. In Revelation 20:13-15 we read of a resurrection of the dead where people will be judged, "And whosoever was not found written in the book of life was cast into the lake of fire." (These are the folks that willingly rejected Jesus, God's only begotten Son, as the sacrifice for their sin.)

When you are "Born Again," your name is written in the "Book of Life." If you name is not there, you are counted with the wicked, no matter what good you may have done while alive.

Being a saint and being "Born Again" is not determined by what you do or do not do. It is determined by what Jesus did. He lived a perfect life in accordance to God's law and as the perfect Lamb of God, without blemish, became the sacrifice on the cross of Calvary, as the penalty for sin. This is the essence of the Gospel or Good News. Paul, the apostle, put it this way, "For by grace (Unmerited Favor) are ye saved through faith; and that not of yourselves: *it is* the gift of God:" Ephesians 2:8

As I mentioned previously, the punishment of the wicked dead in hell is described throughout scripture as "eternal fire" (Matthew 25:41), "unquenchable fire" (Matthew 3:12), "shame and everlasting contempt" (Daniel 12:2), a place where "the fire is not quenched" (Mark 9:44-49), a place of "torment" and "fire" (Luke 16:23-24), "everlasting destruction" (2 Thessalonians 1:9), a place where "the smoke of torment rises forever and ever" (Revelation 14:10-11), and a "lake of burning sulfur" where the wicked are "tormented day and night forever and ever" (Revelation 20:10).

The punishment of the wicked in hell is as never-ending as is the bliss of the righteous in heaven. Jesus himself indicates that punishment in hell is just as everlasting as life in heaven (Matthew 25:46). The wicked are forever subject to the fury and the wrath of God.

Those in hell will acknowledge the perfect justice of God (Psalm 76:10). Those who are in hell will know that their punishment is just and that they alone are to blame (Deuteronomy 32:3-5). Yes, hell is real. Yes, hell is a place of torment and punishment that lasts forever and ever, with no end. Praise God that, through Jesus, we can escape this eternal fate. (John 3:16, 18, 36) Excerpts from GotQuestions.org

WHO ARE THE WICKED?

Will you be numbered with the wicked? Here is what the dictionary said about the word "Wicked" (Highly offensive; obnoxious: a wicked stench.)

- **Adj. wicked** - morally bad in principle or practice.
- **evil** - morally bad or wrong; "evil purposes"; "an evil influence"; "evil deeds" **immoral** - deliberately violating accepted principles of right and wrong **impious** - lacking piety or reverence for a god.
- **wrong** - contrary to conscience or morality or law; "it is wrong for the rich to take advantage of the poor"; "cheating is wrong"; "it is wrong to lie."
- **unrighteous** - not righteous; "an unrighteous man"; "an unrighteous law."

The wicked are people that live in this lifestyle and practice it every day. They violate the laws of God and rebel against his sovereign rule. They are their own god, doing what they want, not what God created them to be.

Here are a few scriptures related to the wicked and their wickedness.

Genesis 6:5 ...” And GOD saw that the wickedness of man was great in the earth, and that every imagination of the thoughts of his heart was only evil continually”.

Genesis 38:7...” And Er, Judah's firstborn, was wicked in the sight of the LORD; and the LORD slew him.”

Chronicles 17:9... “Also, I will ordain a place for my people Israel, and will plant them, and they shall dwell in their place, and shall be moved no more; neither shall the children of wickedness waste them anymore, as at the beginning,”

Habakkuk 1:4 ...” Therefore, the law is slacked, and judgment doth never go forth: for the wicked doth compass about the righteous; therefore, wrong judgment proceeded.”

Malachi 3:18 ...” Then shall ye return, and discern between the righteous and the wicked between him that serves God and him that serves him not.”

Psalms 101:8 ...” I will early destroy all the wicked of the land; that I may cut off all wicked doers from the city of the LORD.”

Proverbs 21:12 ...” The righteous man wisely considers the house of the wicked: but *God* overthrows the wicked for their wickedness.”

Proverbs 21:27 ... “The sacrifice of the wicked *is* abomination: how much more, *when* he bringeth it with a wicked mind?”

WHY ARE THE FIRES OF HELL NECESSARY?

The cleansing fire brings about a complete eradication of sin. Ezekiel

28:18-19 speaks the following about Satan: "Therefore I brought fire from your midst; it devoured you, and I turned you to ashes upon the earth...And (you) shall be no more forever." With Satan and all wickedness burned up, the Bible says that sin and affliction will never arise a second time. (Nahum 1:9)

Peter 3:10-14 explains that earth being on fire will melt, but that we should look forward to a new heaven and a new earth where righteousness dwells. The fire purifies the earth and establishes a place of righteousness for the saved to live. Isaiah 65:17 added, "For behold, I create new heavens and a new earth; and the former shall not be remembered or come to mind."

This righteous place is described in Revelation 21:1-5 in the following way: "Now I saw a new heaven and a new earth, for the first heaven and the first earth had passed away...And God will wipe away every tear from their eyes; there shall be no more death, nor sorrow, nor crying. There shall be no more pain, for the former things have passed away...Then he who sat on the throne said, 'behold, I make all things new.'"

THE REASON HELL WAS CREATED

In a relativistic culture, the very concept of sin must be defended vigorously. If morality is relative to each person, then there is no higher moral standard one can achieve or break.

But as C. S. Lewis argued in *"Mere Christianity"* and *"The Abolition of Man"*, the idea of an objective moral law is inescapable. When we are snubbed or exploited, we call out for justice. When we encounter people of grit and grace, we praise them as moral examples. Our conscience is more than mere instinct or social conditioning. Yet because there is often a great gap between our ideals and actions, we suffer guilt and regret. Despite our denials and excuses, our consciences dog us throughout our days.

Christianity explains the global stain of human guilt by placing it in a theological framework that both sharpens its sting and makes relief possible. Sin is a moral condition that offends the holy God and removes us from his approval.

While much modern psychology assures us that guilt can be gutted through humanistic methods, the Gospel faces the problem head-on. Guilt is real because we have violated the standards of goodness. Left to ourselves, we can do nothing to undo our wrongs.

Forgiving ourselves is never sufficient because we are in no position to exonerate the guilty party — any more than a murderer can grant himself or herself a stay of execution.

Lawbreakers deserve punishment. But is hell too extreme? The great American theologian Jonathan Edwards took this question up in his essay, "The Justice of God in the Damnation of Sinners." Edwards argued that because God is "a Being of infinite greatness, majesty, and glory," He is therefore "infinitely honorable" and worthy of absolute obedience. "Sin against God, being a violation of infinite obligations, must be a crime infinitely heinous, and deserving of infinite punishment."

Edwards's much maligned but solidly Biblical sermon, *"Sinners in the Hands of an Angry God,"* presses home the point that without Christ, we have no grounds for confidence and every reason to fear hell. God, who is angry with sin, could justifiably send the unrepentant sinner to hell at any moment. Jesus himself warned, "Do not be afraid of those who kill the body but cannot kill the soul. Rather, be afraid of the one who can destroy both soul and body in hell" (Matt. 10:28).

To fathom the horror of sin and the holiness of God, we must kneel before the cross of Christ. While the Scriptures command us to be like Christ, this is never presented as the basis of our salvation. Christ's sinless perfection is impossible for us to attain, "for all have sinned and fall short of the glory of God" (Rom. 3:23). Because Jesus flawlessly obeyed God's moral law in our place, he is uniquely qualified to be our Savior. On the cross, Christ offered himself to the Father as a spotless sacrifice for our sin.

Sin against God is so severe that only the death of the sinless Son of God could atone for it. We see the reality of hell when the crucified Christ calls out, "My God, My God, why have you forsaken me?" (Mark 15:34). Paul explains, "God made him who had no sin to be sin for us, so that in him we might become the righteousness of God" (2 Cor. 5:21).

In the cross of Christ, the sinfulness of sin, the holiness of God, and the reality of hell are all seen through the blood of the Lamb. Only through Christ taking on our hell through his death could sinners be reconciled to a holy God. Once this is understood, hell takes on a clarity not otherwise perceived. Apart from the cross, there is no hope for forgiveness or reconciliation. Hell is the only alternative.

Only by understanding hell can we grasp the immensity of God's love. God's love took his Son to the hell of the cross for our sake. This is a costly love, a bloody love that has no parallel in any of the world's religions. Although other religions (particularly Islam) threaten hell, none offer the sure deliverance from it that Christianity offers through the sacrificial love of God himself.

(This article first appeared in the Effective Evangelism column of the CHRISTIAN RESEARCH JOURNAL, volume 19, number 03, 1997.)

For those who do not receive Jesus Christ as Savior, death means everlasting punishment (2 Thessalonians 1:8–9). There is no Biblical support for the notion that after death, people get another chance to repent. Hebrews 9:27 makes it clear that everyone dies physically and, after that, comes the judgment. Christians have already been judged and sentenced. Jesus took that sentence upon himself. Our sin becomes his and his righteousness becomes ours when we believe in him. Because he took our just punishment, we need not fear ever being separated from him again (Romans 8:29–30). The judgment for unbelievers is still to come.

"He will punish those who do not know God and do not obey the gospel of our Lord Jesus. They will be punished with everlasting destruction and shut out from the presence of the Lord and from the glory of his might." II Thessalonians. 1:8-9. The misery of hell will consist of not only physical torture but also the agony of being cut off from every avenue of happiness.

As I said before, God is the source of all good things (James 1:17). To be cut off from God is to forfeit all exposure to anything good. Hell will be a state of perpetual sin; yet those suffering there will possess a full understanding of sin's horrors. Remorse, guilt, and shame will be unending, yet accompanied by the conviction that the punishment is just.

There will no longer be any deception about the "goodness of man." To be separated from God is to be forever shut off from light (1 John 1:5), love (1 John 4:8), joy (Matthew 25:23), and peace (Ephesians 2:14) because God is the source of all those good things. Any good we observe in humanity is merely a reflection of the character of God, in whose image we were created (Genesis 1:27).

While the spirits of those regenerated by God's Holy Spirit will abide forever with God in a perfected state (1 John 3:2), the opposite is true of those in hell. None of the goodness of God will exist in them. Whatever good they may have thought they represented on earth will be shown for the selfish, lustful, idolatrous thing it was (Isaiah 64:6). Man's ideas of goodness will be measured against the perfection of God's holiness and be found severely lacking. Those in hell have forever lost the chance to see God's face, hear His voice, experience His forgiveness, or enjoy his fellowship. To be forever separated from God is the ultimate punishment. (Taken from GotQuestions.com)

THE PLAN OF SALVATION

Old And New Testament Saints

The Old Testament saints put their trust in, "The Coming One" Matt 11:2-7 And when John had heard in prison about the works of Christ, he sent two of his disciples and said to him, "Are You the Coming One, or do we look for another?" Jesus answers and said to them, "Go and tell John the things which you hear and see: the blind see and the lame walk; the lepers are cleansed and the deaf hear; the dead are raised up and the poor have the gospel preached to them. And blessed is he who is not offended because of Me." Isa. 29:18-19 "In that day, the deaf shall hear the words of the book, and the eyes of the blind shall see out of obscurity and out of darkness. The humble also shall increase their joy in the LORD, And the poor among men shall rejoice in the Holy One of Israel. "

THE COMING ONE

Many times, Jesus would make one statement and be quoting or hinting at four or five different verses in the Old Testament, especially when he was being attacked by the religious leaders, he would answer their questions with another question or statement that would allude to the scriptures that they were presuming to know so much about and following so closely. There are many examples, but for now, we will examine John's question and Jesus' response.

If we examine the Old Testament, we will find a multiplicity of statements about the Messiah being regarded as "The Coming One." In Hebrew, its "haba" which means "to come." One of the most popular "Messianic Scriptures" where this word is used is in one of the Psalms: Ps 118:26 "Blessed is he who comes in the name of the LORD!"

Another scripture in the Psalms that was regarded in Judaism as Messianic is in Psalm 40 where it contains the word "haba" spoken by Christ himself through David before Jesus was born: Psalm 40:6-8 Sacrifice and offering You did not desire; My ears you have opened; Burnt offering and sin offering you did not require. Then I said, "Behold, I come; In the scroll of the book, it is written of me. I delight to do your will, O my God, and your law is within my heart."

Another example is found in the last book of our English Bible: Mal 3:1 "Behold, I send my messenger, and he will prepare the way before me. And the Lord, whom you seek, will suddenly come to his temple, even the messenger of the covenant, in whom you delight. Behold, he is coming," said the LORD of hosts.

The knowledge and expectation of the "Coming One" was prevalent during the time of Christ, as we can see from a couple of examples:

John 6:14 "Then those men, when they had seen the sign that Jesus did, said, "This is truly the Prophet who is to come into the world."

John 11:25-27 Jesus said to her, "I am the resurrection and the life. He who believes in Me, though he may die, he shall live. And whoever lives and believes in me shall never die. Do you believe this?" She said to him, "Yes, Lord, I believe that you are the Christ, the Son of God, who is to come into the world."

Old Testament saints looked ahead to the "coming one". Their faith and hope were in him. The New Testament saints looked back to the cross, put their faith in the, "One who came." Messiah is a Hebrew term. It means, "Anointed." and Christ is a Greek term also meaning "Anointed." Thus, both Old and New Testament saints put their trust and faith in the same Anointed One, sent from God. John 3:16 *His Name is Jesus, the Anointed One of God.*

Now all the folks that never heard of this "Anointed One", which Jesus proved he was, fall into the Romans 2:14-15 "Salvation Net" that is stated above. All babies and children under the age of accountability are automatically saved because they have not willfully denied God's plan of salvation.

God does not want anyone to go to hell (2 Peter 3:9). That is why God made the ultimate, perfect, and sufficient sacrifice on our behalf. So, how can we not go to hell? Since only an infinite and eternal penalty is sufficient, an infinite and eternal price must be paid.

God became a human being in the person of Jesus Christ (John 1:1, 14). In Jesus Christ, God lived among us, taught us, and healed us—but those things were not his ultimate mission. God became a human being so that he could die for us. Jesus, God in human form, died on the cross.

As God, his death was infinite and eternal in value, paying the full price for sin (1 John 2:2). God invites us to receive Jesus Christ as Savior, accepting his death as the full and just payment for our sins. God promises that anyone who believes in Jesus (John 3:16), trusting him alone as the Savior (John 14:6), will be saved, i.e., not go to hell.

WHAT ABOUT THE GENTILES... (EVERYONE ELSE)

"For when the Gentiles, which have not the law, do by nature the things contained in the law, these, having not the law, are a law unto themselves: Which shew the work of the law written in their hearts, their conscience also bearing witness, and their thoughts the meanwhile accusing or else excusing one another" Romans 2:14-15 We have already discussed this in chapter five.

If you want this salvation, repent of your sin, and receive Jesus as your Savior. It is as simple as that. Tell God that you recognize you are a sinner and that you deserve to go to hell. Declare to God that you are trusting in Jesus Christ as your Savior. Thank God for providing for your salvation and deliverance from hell. Simple faith, trusting in Jesus Christ as the Savior, is how you can avoid going to hell!

Yes, God is sovereign. He Lords over everything in his creation. Hell is not exempt from God's sovereign rule. We should be cognizant of why hell exists and be sure we do not make free will choices that take us there.

CHAPTER TEN: THE SOVEREIGNTY OF GOD AND YOUR EVERY DAY.

Make no mistake, my friends, God is sovereign over your every day. He has a plan for your life and a destiny that he wants you to see and attain. That destiny will require your full cooperation. He takes no prisoners, and he does not drag anyone down the road to glory. You will have to fight the good fight of faith to get there.

Fighting the good fight of faith simply means that we will not consider Christ's sacrifice as nothing. Fighting the good fight of faith means that we will value what Christ has given to us higher than any other thing in this universe, even larger than our very lives, and we will fight for it, no matter what.

Fighting the good fight of faith is to be steadfast in our beliefs with no compromise when faced with false doctrines, fake Christians and persecution from liberals that serve the god of this world.

Fighting the good fight of faith is about **making a choice**; a choice to pursue God's will and a life of faith daily. It is about deciding to fight the temptations and factors that pull us away from God.

Paul told us it's about the Christian faith and the battleground for the fight is about preserving the faith just like Jude wrote, "contend for the faith that was once for all delivered to the saints" (Jude 1:3). The faith that has already been delivered runs from Genesis to Revelation. There is a battle going on; a battle for the truth, so we must strive to preserve what has already been delivered to the saints. We are not expecting any new deliveries because it was "once for all delivered."

Our fight for the faith makes us stronger in the faith. James wrote "For you know that the testing of your faith produces steadfastness" (James 1:3) so the testing of our faith, in fighting for the faith once delivered, produces a steadfastness for the Christian, so keep fighting the good fight of faith.

The very best possible fighting position that a believer could possibly take is on his or her knees because "The LORD will fight for you, and you have only to be silent" (Ex 14:14); in this way, God receives all the glory

Here are four very important Bible verses about fighting the good fight of faith. Offered by Jack Wellman, pastor of Heritage Evangelical Free Church in Udall, KS

- **2 Timothy 4:7 "I have fought the good fight, I have finished the race, I have kept the faith."**

The 2nd Book of Timothy and chapter four might be one of the most heartbreaking chapters for me to read. For one thing, Paul wrote, "I am already being poured out as a drink offering, and the time of my departure has come. I have fought the good fight, I have finished the race, I have kept the faith" (2 Tim 4:6-7) so he knew he was about to die and even though "Demas, in love with this present world, has deserted me and gone to Thessalonica. Luke alone is with me" (2 Tim 4:10-11a).

Paul wrote that *"At my first defense no one came to stand by me, but all deserted me. May it not be charged against them"*

(2 Tim 4:16) so in the end, all had forsaken him but only "the Lord stood by me and strengthened me, so that through me the message might be fully proclaimed and all the Gentiles might hear it. So, I was rescued from

the lion's mouth. The Lord will rescue me from every evil deed and bring me safely into his heavenly kingdom. To him be the glory forever and ever. Amen." (2 Tim 4:17-18).

- **1 Timothy 6:12 "Fight the good fight of the faith. Take hold of the eternal life to which you were called and about which you made the good confession in the presence of many witnesses."**

This is one of the clearest commands in the Bible that we are to fight the good fight of faith, but what is this fight about?

- **Ephesians 6:12 "For we do not wrestle against flesh and blood, but against the rulers, against the authorities, against the cosmic powers over this present darkness, against the spiritual forces of evil in the heavenly places."**

Jacob wrestled with God, but he had been wrestling with a lot of others before this. His name means "supplanter" or "deceiver." After Jacob had wrestled with God, he realized that *"I have seen God face to face, and yet my life has been delivered"* (Gen 32:20). Jacob's name was later changed to Israel as God said, *"you have striven with God and with men, and have prevailed"* (Gen 32:28).

Today, we wrestle against an unseen enemy. Satan and his demons are spirit beings but very powerful ones too and because of this, it is necessary to put on *"the whole armor of God, that you may be able to stand against the schemes of the devil"* (Eph 6:11).

- **James 1:12 "Blessed is the man who remains steadfast under trial, for when he has stood the test, he will receive the crown of life, which God has promised to those who love him."**

How blessed is the man or woman who remains firm in their faith, remaining steadfast even under trials. Just as God told ancient Israel, *"You shall not fear them, for it is the LORD your God who fights for you"* (Deut. 3:22).

The things we fear the most, like trials, financial difficulties, and relationship problems, are best handled by letting God handle them. Commit it to prayer and then commit it to God because he alone can direct even a pagan king's heart (Prov 21:1) so do not be like *"those who shrink back and are destroyed, but of those who have faith and preserve their souls"* (Heb 10:39).

Fighting the good fight of faith is to... "Take hold of the eternal life to which you were called when you made your good confession in the presence of many witnesses" (1 Timothy 6:12, NIV)

We seek after it until we capture it and then we do not let it go. The thing we go after to capture is the gospel of Jesus Christ. This is where we discover salvation and the hope of eternal life and the fellowship of the Spirit and the grace of God. We are ever mindful of its power and blessings that befall those that are exercised by it.

We must stand firm in our faith, knowing that we are the children of God and have overcome them: because greater is he that is in us, than he that is in the world." John 4:4

The battle is the Lord's and we have the joy of ruling with him until all is finished and peace is restored in God's kingdom.

If you are a" Born Again" believer, you have the Holy Spirit dwelling inside of you. "What? know ye not that your body is the temple of the Holy Ghost which is in you, which ye have of God, and ye are not your own?" I Corinthians 6:19.

If the Holy Spirit really dwells in you, he is greater than anyone or any spirit, even Satan. "You are of God, little children, and have overcome them, because he who is in you is greater than he who is in the world. One greater than every demon, storm, trial, lack, attack, or depression is living in you today. He is more powerful than any sickness, disease, or affliction." I John 4:4 Are we in agreement so far?

If you are walking with the Lord, being filled with his Spirit, you have spiritual authority. Here are a few Bible references related to the believer's authority.

Mark 16:17 ...And these signs will accompany those who believe: in my name they will cast out demons; they will speak in new tongues;

James 4:7 ...Submit yourselves therefore to God. Resist the devil, and he will flee from you.

Luke 10:19 ...Behold, I have given you authority to tread on serpents and scorpions, and over all the power of the enemy, and nothing shall hurt you.

Matthew 16:19 ...I will give you the keys of the kingdom of heaven, and whatever you bind on earth shall be bound in heaven, and whatever you loose on earth shall be loosed in heaven."

1 Peter 5:8 ...Be sober-minded; be watchful. Your adversary, the devil, prowls around like a roaring lion, seeking someone to devour.

Luke 10:19-21 ...Behold, I have given you authority to tread on serpents and scorpions, and over all the power of the enemy, and nothing shall hurt you. Nevertheless, do not rejoice in this, that the spirits are subject to you, but rejoice that your names are written in heaven. In that same hour, he rejoiced in the Holy Spirit and said, "I thank you, Father, Lord of heaven and earth, that you have hidden these things from the wise and understanding and revealed them to little children; yes, Father, for such was your gracious will."

1 John 4:4 ... Little children, you are from God and have overcome them, for he who is in you is greater than he who is in the world.

Revelation 12:11 ...And they have conquered him by the blood of the Lamb and by the word of their testimony, for they loved not their lives even unto death.

Mark 11:23 ...Truly, I say to you, whoever say to this mountain, 'Be taken up and thrown into the sea,' and does not doubt in his heart, but believes that what he said will come to pass, it will be done for him.

Hebrews 4:12 ... For the word of God is living and active, sharper than any two-edged sword, piercing to the division of soul and of spirit, of joints and of marrow, and discerning the thoughts and intentions of the heart.

Acts 1:8 ... But you will receive power when the Holy Spirit has come upon you, "and you will be my witnesses in Jerusalem and in all Judea and Samaria, and to the end of the earth."

John 14:12 ..."Truly, truly, I say to you, whoever believes in me will also do the works that I do; and greater works than these will he do, because I am going to the Father."

Luke 10:17-19 ... The seventy-two returned with joy, saying, "Lord, even the demons are subject to us in your name!" And he said to them, "I saw Satan fall like lightning from heaven. Behold, I have given you authority to tread on serpents and scorpions, and over all the power of the enemy, and nothing shall hurt you."

Mark 6:13 ... And they cast out many demons and anointed with oil, many who were sick and healed them.

Ephesians 6:10-18 ... Finally, be strong in the Lord and in the strength of his might. Put on the whole armor of God, that you may be able to stand against the schemes of the devil. For we do not wrestle against flesh and blood, but against the rulers, against the authorities, against the cosmic powers over this present darkness, against the spiritual forces of evil in the heavenly places. Therefore, take up the whole armor of God, that you may be able to withstand in the evil day, and having done all, to stand firm. Stand therefore, having fastened on the belt of truth, and having put on the breastplate of righteousness.

Matthew 28:18-20 ... And Jesus came and said to them, "All authority in heaven and on earth has been given to me. Go therefore and make disciples of all nations, baptizing them in the name of the Father and of the Son and of the Holy Spirit, teaching them to observe all that I have commanded you. And behold, I am with you always, to the end of the age."

Psalm 91:13 ... You will tread on the lion and the adder; the young lion and the serpent you will trample underfoot.

Acts 2:39 ... For the promise is for you and for your children and for all who are far off, everyone whom the Lord our God calls to himself.

Matthew 10:1 ... And he called to him his twelve disciples and gave them authority over unclean spirits, to cast them out, and to heal every disease and every affliction.

Acts 16:18 ... And this she kept doing for many days. Paul, having become greatly annoyed, turned and said to the spirit, "I command you in the name of Jesus Christ to come out of her." And it came out that very hour.

Acts 3:6 ... But Peter said, "I have no silver and gold, but what I do have I give to you. In the name of Jesus Christ of Nazareth, rise up and walk!"

Luke 10:1-42 ... After this, the Lord appointed seventy-two others and sent them on ahead of him, two by two, into every town and place where he himself was about to go. And he said to them, "The harvest is plentiful, but the laborers are few. Therefore, pray earnestly to the Lord of the harvest to send out laborers into his harvest. Go your way; behold, I am sending you out as lambs in the midst of wolves. Carry no moneybag, no knapsack, no sandals, and greet no one on the road. Whatever house you enter, first say, 'Peace be to this house!' ...

Acts 2:1-47 ... When the day of Pentecost arrived; they were all together in one place. And suddenly there came from heaven a sound like a mighty rushing wind, and it filled the entire house where they were sitting. And divided tongues as of fire appeared to them and rested on each one of them. And they were all filled with the Holy Spirit and began to speak in other tongues as the Spirit gave them utterance. Now there were dwelling in Jerusalem, Jews, devout men from every nation under heaven. ...

Revelation 12:10 ... And I heard a loud voice in heaven, said, "Now the salvation and the power and the kingdom of our God and the authority of his Christ have come, for the accuser of our brothers has been thrown down, who accuses them day and night before our God."

1 Corinthians 12:8 ... For to one is given through the Spirit the utterance of wisdom, and to another the utterance of knowledge according to the same Spirit,

We have the Spiritual authority or power of Jesus at our disposal. We can use it or not. If we do not, we will remain defeated and live in a carnal world, being plagued by evil forces at every turn. It is far more to our advantage to stand up in the Lord and the power of his might and declare our freedom and walk in his will.

As in most promises of God, it is up to us. God will not invade our free will. He will sit quietly by and watch us fall and then pick us up and start again to teach our hands to war so we can be victorious.

I Am A Believer & I Have Authority To Spoil The Works of The Devil

When you believe, you rely upon, you adhere to, and you trust in. That, my friends, is believing with the heart. That is what is necessary to overcome the rulers of darkness and win the battle. This is fighting the good fight of faith.

We are encouraged by them to "Walk by Faith and Not by Sight." 2 Corinthians 5:7

The Bible says we are to fight the good fight. That suggests that there is also a bad fight. One can fight badly or outside of proper battle tactics. Hitler did that when he sent 29-million people to the gas chambers in WWII.

We want to use tactics that God has set up for us so we are assured of victory. If we run off in the flesh to fight a spiritual enemy, we will fail. That is doing things in bad form. It is not a good fight. The good fight of faith is a spiritual fight with spiritual weapons that have been provided by God for our use.

We must put on the entire armor of God and stand fast in the liberty Jesus gained for us on the cross. We must walk in the Spirit so we do not glorify the flesh. The deeds of the flesh will kill us over time. They tend to degrade our personalities, destroy our self-esteem, and cause sadness, depression, and guilt.

Remember, we do not fight with flesh and blood, but rather with the rulers of darkness and spiritual wickedness in high places.

Jesus has already won this battle. All we need to do is stand fast, resist and take authority over all that is anti-Christ. If God is with us, who can be against us? No one that can win, for we are already more than conquerors in Christ Jesus.

Remember, God is sovereign and all powerful. He has given us a free will. However, that freedom is given so we can choose to rule over our everyday experiences and live in abundance of joy, peace and all the other fruits of his Spirit.

It's time to fight the good fight of faith

CONCLUSION

It is your choice. Do not allow anyone to take the God-given power of choice away from you. Remember, God created man in his image and likeness. God did not create man as a robotic toy for his playtime. You have received and still possess the gift of free will, and God expects you to exercise your freedom of choice in ways that will glorify him.

However, remember that free will comes with accountability. "Be not deceived; God is not mocked: for whatsoever a man soweth, that shall he also reap." Galatians 6:7. That means we should not use our free will (Power of choice) to choose abortion or other immoral actions. We plant evil and evil will grow up and strangle us.

We must use our minds to discern the word of God and add to that simple common sense and practical logic to draw accurate conclusions. Here are some logical conclusions I have reasoned over the past 60+ years:

"God is no respecter of persons." Acts 10:34 This means that God does not show favoritism to anyone based upon their status, race, or sin.. The same scripture is also quoted in Romans 2:11, where it is followed by the explanation that all have sinned and will be judged by God's law. God expects his people to follow his example and not respect persons in judgment, but to be fair and righteous.

The Spirit of adoption witnesses with our spirit that we are his children. "For ye have not received the spirit of bondage again to fear; but ye have received the Spirit of adoption, whereby we cry, Abba, Father. The

Spirit itself bears witness with our spirit, that we are the children of God:" Romans 8:15-16.

- ***The offer of salvation extends to all humanity.*** "For God so loved the world that he gave his only begotten Son, that whosoever believes in him should have everlasting life." John 3:16.

- ***Jesus receives everyone who accepts the Father's call to salvation, and he does not cast any of them out.*** "All that the Father gives me shall come to me; and him that comes to me I will in no wise cast out." John 6:37.

- ***Salvation comes to us by God's good grace, and it is received by our faith in the finished work of Christ on the cross. "For*** by grace are ye saved through faith; and that not of yourselves: it is the gift of God: not of works, lest any man should boast." Ephesian 2:8-9.

I am sure you will read other scriptures that show the truth of the gospel. Keep searching, keep knocking on the door of heaven and keep asking the Holy Spirit to show you all things.

Some people emphasize the sovereignty of God to the point where they believe human beings are little more than robots, simply carrying out what they have been sovereignly programmed to do.

Others emphasize free will to the point of God not having complete control and/or knowledge of all things. Neither of these positions is biblical. The truth is that God does not violate our wills by choosing us and redeeming us. Rather, He changes our hearts so that our wills choose him. "We love hm because he first loved us" (1 John 4:19), and "You did not choose me, but I chose you" (John 15:16).

What are we to do then?

First, we are to trust in the Lord, knowing that he is in control (Proverbs

3:5-6). God's sovereignty is supposed to be a comfort to us, not an issue to be concerned about or debated.

Second, we are to live our lives making wise decisions in accordance with God's Word (2 Timothy 3:16-17; James 1:5). There will be no excuses before God for why we disobeyed him. We will have no one to blame but ourselves for our sin.

Finally, we are to worship the Lord, praising him that he is so wonderful, infinite, powerful, full of grace and mercy—and sovereign. (Excerpts from gotquestions.com)

One last comment... I do not subscribe to either the Calvinistic viewpoint or the Arminian. They both border on heresy. I would rather serve the Lord by walking in the Spirit and follow Jesus without all the expectations of man's doctrines. I see most of them as heretical teaching that will lead true seekers away from the truth.

ABOUT THE AUTHOR

Rev. Marinelli is an ordained minister, He has formed and been pastor of one church in Wisconsin and was the pastor of another in Alabama. He has also been a youth minister and evangelism director over the years.

Rev. Marinelli has authored over 30-books that can be viewed on his website:

www.marrinellichristianbooks.com

John is an accomplished Christian poet. He also dabbles in songwriting and writing one act Christian plays. He is the Vice President of Have A Heart For Companion Animals, Inc., a "No Kill" animal welfare organization. He volunteers his time promoting fundraising events for www.haveaheartusa.org.

Rev. Marinelli is now retired from the sales and marketing arena after spending over 40 years in business-to-business and non-profit marketing. He enjoys writing Christian themed books, playing chess, singing karaoke and a retired lifestyle in sunny Florida

For More Info eMail Contact **johnmarinelli@embarqmail.com**

SELECTED CHRISTIAN POETRY BY JOHN MARINELLI, THE AUTHOR

"I AM" THERE

"I AM" There,
At the end of your broken dreams,
Before the sun rises over your day,
Prior to those tear-filled streams.

"I AM" There,
Down that road of despair,
When all appears to be lost,
And no one seems to care.

"I AM" There,
Over all of life's twists and turns,
When tomorrow is all but gone,
And when you are full of concerns.

"I AM" There,
Sayeth the Lord of Host,
To bring you hope and peace,
And the power of my Holy Ghost.

"I AM" There,
To be sure you make it through,
In the midst of every trial,
To bless your life and deliver you.

"I Am" There

"All power is given unto me in heaven and earth. Go ye therefore and teach all nations, baptizing them in the name of the Father, and of the Son, and of the Holy Ghost: Teaching them to observe all things, whatsoever I have commanded you: and lo, I am with you always, even unto the end of the world." Mathew 28:18-20

The Lord is with us always. He never leaves our side, even when we leave His. In every situation, He is there. It's time to count on His presence and trust in His grace.

GUARDIAN ANGEL

The Angel of the Lord
Comes with a mighty army,
To fight the enemies of God.

Then he opens our eyes
That we might see the battle
And walk where angels trod.

Our guardian angels
Beholds the very face of God,
Standing there on our behalf.

Our guardian angels
Are ready with God's power,
To quiet evil's awful wrath.

"Take heed that ye despise not one of these little ones; for I say unto you, That in heaven, there angels do always behold the face of my Father, which is in heaven" Mathew 18:10

As God's children, we have guardian angels that watch over us and report back to God. They are ministering spirits especially placed in service to help the saints on their way to glory.

THE ANGEL'S CAMP

The angel of the Lord
Sets up his camp
Around those that reverence God.

Imagine being there
In the midst of
Where angels trod.

What a joy it is
To know God's protection
And to be in the angel's camp.

It is there that God's children
Are delivered from evil's woe
And led by heaven's lamp.

" The angel of the Lord encamps round about them that fear Him, and delivers them" Psalm 34:7

Deliverance come through reverence and respect for God and a belief that He will be there with His angels to help you in times of trouble.

ALL CREATION WAITS

A blue-gray sky
Winks at the dawn,
As the morning light
Sings its glorious song.

Life is flourishing everywhere,
Unaware of what's in store.
The sounds of spring beckons,
In a silent and peaceful roar.

Time marches onward,
Towards the brink of day,
As all of creation waits
For God's children to pray.

It's time to stand up and be counted as a child of God. It's time to pray for peace and deliverance. Creation is waiting.

DON'T WORRY

Don't worry about tomorrow.
You did that yesterday.
Go on with your life
And remember always to pray.

Ask and it shall be given to you,
But this great truth you already know.
Rejoice and be happy, why? Because…
Your harvest comes from what you sow.

I will say it again and even more,
Until it becomes very very clear.
Tomorrow will take care of itself,
But worry is another word for fear.

Now here's what I want you to do.
Trust in the Lord and be of good cheer.
Drop the worry from your vocabulary
And cast out that demon of fear.

Worry is a sin so stop it. Be of good cheer. It's all up to you. Life is too short to spend it worrying.

ARM'S LENGTH

I hold the world at arm's length,
That its choices do not interfere.
While it does its own thing,
I watch and wait over here.

My steps must not go that way,
For it's not where I need to be.
The Lord has shown me the path,
That will lead me to my destiny.

The call to follow sin is strong
And pulls at me now and then.
But I know that way
Is full of sorrow and sin.

I must move on in life
Beyond their beckoning call.
It's the right thing to do,
So I do not stumble or fall.

I will not be swayed or misled
By family, friends or business deal.
Their secret thoughts are not mine,
To consider, to admire or feel.
So I keep the world at "Arm's Length"
As I journey through this life.
My faith in Jesus keeps me strong,
As I walk in His glorious light.

Arm's length is a good policy. Be sure you stay in the Lord and close to Him. It's the only way to keep sane in such a crazy world.

CLUTTER

Clutter keeps the mind confused,
As images dance through the night.
Lost among those unimportant thoughts,
Are the dreams that once shined bright.

An endless parade of fear and doubt,
Crowds the mind to destroy our day.
Ever soaring on the wings of the soul,
Until it has formed an evil array.

But clutter is by one's choice,
Of those who dance to its beat.
Better to face imaginations' due
Than to fall into utter defeat.

Set up a filter that keeps out unnecessary thoughts. A good practice is to go by the still waters in your mind and rest there until the flow of life situations becomes manageable.

I FIND MYSELF IN GOD

I find myself in God.
He is my "everything"
I know that He is Lord,
My Life, my Hope, and King.

I find myself in God,
Not the ways of sin.
Nor do I look to others,
To know who I really am.

I find myself in God,
To whom I bow on bended knee.
He alone is my joy and strength
And where I want to be.

You cannot really know yourself unless you first know God. He created you in His images and until you discover Him, you will never find yourself.

THE ANGELS CRY "HOLY,"

The Angels cry "Holy,"
While sorrow fills the land.
For God's Judgment Day,
Is to come upon every man.

The Angels cry "Holy,"
While mankind goes astray,
Rejecting the love of God,
To follow his own precarious way.

The Angels cry "Holy,"
Knowing the terror of the Lord,
When all who dwell in sin,
Will suddenly be destroyed.

The Angels cry "Holy,"
Waiting for all things new,
Born of the Holy Spirit,
When God's Judgment is through.

The Angels cry "Holy,"
"Holy is the Lamb,"
Waiting for the children of God,
To join "The Great I AM"

Heaven is waiting for us to join our Savior. What a great day that will be.
Are you ready? I am.

REST MY CHILD

Take your peace and be restored
Then put your faith in Jesus, the Lord
He has provided, your mouth to feed.
From the beginning, He knew your need.

Do not worry, fret or even fear,
for, my child, He is always near.
To bless your soul with love and grace,
To be with you, face to face.

Come, my child, near to His throne.
Do not allow your faith to roam.
For those who will not believe,
Can never find rest in times of need.

His word shall see you through.
His grace He freely gives to you.
That you should rest, your soul to keep,
Forever delivered from unbelief.

Go ahead, rest in the Lord. I dare you. It may be scary at first but it sure feels good when you get use to it.

WINNING THE BATTLE

We must use the Word of God
To calm emotions that fray.
For the enemy never sleeps,
Until he has led us astray.

So when your emotions overflow
With feelings like depression and fear.
Know this! If you dwell in that place,
You invite the enemy to draw near.

When your emotions rage
With fiery darts aglow,
Stand in the power of the Lord,
Against its awful woe.

And if you get confused
And lost in the storm,
Put your thoughts on trial,
Rejecting all but heaven born.

You can win the battle
That rages within your soul.
By casting down imaginations,
And breaking Satan's hold.
Remember to focus on Jesus,
Holding the world at arm's length.
Lift up your head above the trial,
And the Lord will give you strength.

"For the weapons of our warfare are not carnal but mighty, through God, to the pulling down of strongholds: casting down imaginations and every high thing that exalts itself against the knowledge of God, and bringing into captivity every thought to the obedience of Christ." II Corinthians 10:3-5 The battle is in our minds and we win by putting our thoughts on trial and casting out all that oppose the knowledge of God. This is true victory.

LITTLE PRISONS

Little prisons await the man with a lustful soul.
Bars of selfishness and pride create dungeons of icy cold.

Prisons of shame and jealousy fill the heart with utter despair.
Bars that separate from God and those that really care.

Stand back! While the doors are tightly closed;
Taking away your life, to wither as a dying rose.

Beware of those little prisons that trap the lustful soul.
Keep yourself free from sin through faith in the Christ of old.

Little prisons need not to be your fate.
It is your choice, Spirit or flesh to date.

"O Foolish Galatians, who hath bewitched you, that ye should not obey the truth, before whose eyes Jesus Christ hath been, evidently set forth, crucified among you? Are you so foolish? Having begun in the Spirit, are you now made perfect in the flesh?

We should always seek to dwell in the Spirit, that we would not emulate the deeds of the flesh. When we fall short, we create "little prisons" that keep us in confusion and away from the blessing of God. It's time to walk in the Spirit and break the prisons that so easily beset us

THE WRESTLING MATCH

We wrestle not with flesh and blood,
For man is not our enemy.
Instead, we fight demons in the spirit
That seek to steal our destiny.

But our weapons are not earthly,
Like tanks, guns or bombs.
Instead, we "Plead The Blood"
And shout our victory songs.

So do not wrestle with humanity
Even though evil is there.
Go after Satan, the real enemy
And strip his kingdom bare.

"For though we walk in the flesh, we do not war after the flesh: for the weapons of our warfare are not carnal but mighty, through God, to the pulling down of strongholds; casting down imaginations and every high thing that exalts itself above the knowledge of God, and bring into captivity, every thought to the obedience of Christ." II Corinthians 10: 3-6

Don't fight with other people. Just go about your own business, counting on God to be the avenger. He is the one that holds all the power and strength. If we fight in the flesh, we can fall to strongholds and demons. But standing up in the Spirit and using the name of Jesus, applying the knowledge of God in the situation and casting down every ungodly imagination, will always lead us to victory.

OH' THE BLOOD

Oh, the blood of Jesus
That washed away my sin.
What a great blessing
To have God as my friend.

This one thing I know for sure,
That when I confess my sin,
His cleansing blood will flow,
And I can walk again with Him.

Oh, the blood of Jesus,
How great a sacrifice for me.
For it was the blood of the Lamb
That healed my soul and set me free.

"If we confess our sins, he is faithful and just to forgive us our sins and to cleanse us from all unrighteousness." I John 1:9

It is the blood of Jesus that is the cleansing agent in forgiveness, acceptance by God and salvation of the soul. Without His blood, there would be no payment for sin. Saint John, in chapter three, says that the wages for sin is death. Jesus paid the price so we could go free to serve God, the Father.

ONE MAN

It was by one man, Adam,
That the world fell into sin.
He chose to disobey God's word
And lost God's Spirit within.

No more walks with God
Through the garden of God's grace.
No more close up and personal
To walk along and talk, face to face.

One man, Adam, gave up
The very nature of God.
Never again to stroll along
Where angels once trod.

Evil now flows through his blood
Where only righteousness was before.
He gave up the Spirit of life
To open up death's awful door.

But one Man, Jesus, came from God
To seek and to save that which was lost.
The life of God in man, once again,
Because He paid sin's incredible cost.

" Therefore, as by one man, sin entered into the world, and death by sin; and so death passed upon all men, for that all have sinned. For as by one man's disobedience, many were made sinners, so by the obedience of one, many shall be made righteous." Romans 5:12 & 19

Adam fell and lost the Spirit of God inside of him because of his disobedience; But Jesus obeyed, did not fall and restored what Adam lost. All die in Adam because of sin but all who believe in Jesus shall live in Christ because of His righteousness.

IN THE FULLNESS OF TIME

In the fullness of time,
Jesus came, made of a woman.
Our Heavenly Father sent Him
Because our adoption was at hand.

He was born under the law,
So He might redeem us from it,
And to receive adoption as sons,
Being children of God, we sit.

We who God made His children,
Have the Spirit of His Son,
Deep within our heart of hearts,
So we can finally become one.

"But when the fullness of time was come, God sent forth his son, made of a woman, made under the law, to redeem them that were under the law, that we might receive the adoption of sons. And because we are sons, God has sent forth the spirit of his son into our hearts, crying, Abba, Father." Galatians 4:4-6

We are the adopted sons of God. We, like no other, have the indwelling presence of the Spirit of His Son, who cries out unto God the Father. If your spirit is not crying out to God, you may want to find out why?

FRAGILE FLOWER RED

As a flower in earthen sod,
I bloom for thee, oh God.
To blossom with the turn of spring;
To be to you, a beautiful thing.

I lift my Fragile Flower Red
Upward from my earthen bed;
To draw light from God above,
Strength and peace and joy and love.

As a flower, I bloom for thee
That passersby may stop and see.
Your fragrance and beauty I am,
Flowered in grace as a man.

As a flower in earthen sod,
I bloom for thee, oh God.
Upward, I lift my head,
As a Fragile Flower Red.

"Be not conformed to this world, but be ye transformed, by the renewing of your mind, that ye may prove what is that good and acceptable and perfect will of God."

When we look to God as our source, we blossom, much like a flower that draws light from the sun. When we blossom, like a flower, we display the glory and beauty of our creator to all who care to stop and look. This is our divine providence.

www.ingramcontent.com/pod-product-compliance
Lightning Source LLC
Chambersburg PA
CBHW022031150726
47990CB00002B/904